# YORK NOT[

*General Editors:* Professor
*of Stirling*) & Professor Su
*University of Beirut*)

CW00502753

## J.R.R. Tolkien

# THE HOBBIT

*Notes by Geoffrey M. Ridden*

BA M PHIL (LEEDS)
*Senior Lecturer in English,*
*King Alfred's College, Winchester*

LONGMAN
YORK PRESS

YORK PRESS
Immeuble Esseily, Place Riad Solh, Beirut.

LONGMAN GROUP LIMITED
Burnt Mill,
Harlow, Essex

© Librairie du Liban 1981

*All rights reserved. No part of this publication may be reproduced,
stored in a retrieval system, or transmitted in any form or by any
means, electronic, mechanical, photocopying, recording, or otherwise,
without the prior permission of the copyright owner.*

First published 1981
ISBN 0 582 78230 9

Printed in Hong Kong by
Wilture Enterprises (International) Ltd.

# Contents

# Part 1

# Introduction

## The author

John Ronald Reuel Tolkien was born on 3 January 1892 in Bloem-
fontein, South Africa, where his father was a bank manager. While the
young Tolkien was in England with his mother and younger brother in
1896, his father died, and the family settled in England. He was taught
by his mother in Worcestershire before winning a scholarship at King
Edward's School in nearby Birmingham in 1903. On his mother's death
in 1904 Father Francis Morgan became his guardian and Tolkien
remained a practising Roman Catholic throughout his life.

In 1910 Tolkien won an exhibition at Exeter College, Oxford. Here
he came under the influence of Joseph Wright, a scholar with a particular interest in the history of the English language and in medieval
literature. Tolkien spent much of his time working on the invention of
an 'Elvish language' and an accompanying Elvish mythology.

After leaving Oxford with a First Class degree in English he served
in the Army with the Lancashire Fusiliers until he was invalided out in
1918. He had married Edith Mary Bratt in 1916, and they subsequently
had four children: a daughter and three sons.

Tolkien worked for two years as an Assistant on the Oxford English
Dictionary before entering academic life at the University of Leeds in
1920. He was to be associated with academic scholarship for the re-
mainder of his life. He became Professor of English Language at Leeds
in 1924, and in the following year he was appointed Rawlinson and
Bosworth Professor of Anglo-Saxon at Oxford, a post he held for
twenty years. In 1945 he became Merton Professor of English Language
and Literature and, on his retirement in 1959, he was elected an
Emeritus Fellow of Merton College.

Tolkien was a scholar of great repute, specialising in the literature of
medieval England and, in particular, that part of England where he had
spent much of his boyhood. The dialect of the West Midlands is the
most obscure dialect of the medieval period but it contains one of the
period's greatest poems, *Sir Gawain and the Green Knight*, and Tolkien's
edition of this poem (which he undertook in collaboration with E.V.
Gordon in 1925) did much to make the work accessible to modern
readers. It remains the standard edition even today.

In 1936 Tolkien delivered a lecture on the Old English poem *Beowulf* (composed in the early eighth century) which became the touchstone of a new method of approaching the poem: encouraging readers to try to understand it as a piece of literature rather than as a storehouse of historical material. In the same year that this lecture was published (1937) Tolkien's first novel, *The Hobbit*, came into print. Even before its publication Tolkien had started to work on a much more ambitious romance which, although including hobbits, dwarves, elves, and goblins, is far from being a sequel to *The Hobbit*. The trilogy *The Lord of the Rings*, which was published in three volumes between 1954 and 1956, is not addressed to children in the way that *The Hobbit* is; and its central object, the ring, is more of a symbol of the corruptibility of all creatures than the device to confer invisibility which we find in *The Hobbit*.

Tolkien's fantasies gained him a world-wide popularity and led to the publication of other stories and verses for children, and to an increasing demand for him to complete the work which had been in his mind since he was an undergraduate: the Elvish myth into which *The Hobbit* and *The Lord of the Rings* were intended to slot, the story of a beautiful elf-woman and her mortal lover, *The Silmarillion*. This work was still incomplete when Tolkien died on 2 September 1973, and it was left to Christopher Tolkien to edit his father's papers and to publish the long-awaited work in 1977.

# Fairy tales and fantasy

The first edition of *The Hobbit* was an immediate popular success both in England and in the United States of America. It has been reprinted many times and is currently available in some twenty different languages. Tolkien's work, especially *The Lord of the Rings*, has received widespread critical attention (R.C. West's list of Tolkien criticism included 196 items by 1970*). Nevertheless, it is necessary to remember that *The Hobbit* was intended to be read by children and not by critics, and it is worth investigating the reasons which led an Oxford professor to publish a children's story.

In a lecture which he delivered in 1938, Tolkien spoke of the way in which stories involving enchantment had come to be regarded as trivial, suitable only to be adapted for children. This, he felt, did justice neither to the stories nor to the children, and he went on to define what he considered to be the strengths of 'fairy-stories'. Dismissing the relatively modern idea of fairies being tiny, silly creatures, he treated stories about *Faerie* ('the realm or state in which fairies have their being') as part of

*R.C. WEST: *Tolkien Criticism: An Annotated Checklist*, Kent State University Press, Kent, Ohio, 1970.

a kind of fantasy which allowed readers to move from the prison of their normal lives and to 'survey the depths of space and time'. In order to be successful he felt that such stories had to be presented seriously and the writer or story maker had to become 'a successful "sub-creator". He makes a Secondary World which your mind can enter. Inside it, what he relates is "true": it accords with the laws of that world.'* In addition to the Fantasy of this Secondary World, a fairy-story should, he said, offer the reader the further features of Recovery (a new sense of seeing fundamentals quite clearly); Escape from the confines of one's own life; and the Consolation of a happy ending.

The ideas that Tolkien was advancing in this lecture were largely shared by a group of Oxford scholars and friends who banded together in the late 1930s to form a literary circle called The Inklings. This group met on Thursday evenings to talk, smoke, drink beer, and to read aloud from their writing; it was to this circle of friends that Tolkien read the first drafts of *The Hobbit*, at a time when the only other people who knew of the story's existence were his own family.

The central figure in The Inklings was C.S. Lewis (1898-1963); and it is an indication of the significance and seriousness which this group attributed to fantasy literature that Lewis himself became a practising Christian after Tolkien explained to him the mythical qualities of the story of the death of Jesus Christ. The Inklings in general, and Tolkien in particular, were seeking a renewed sense of spiritual consciousness to compensate for the inadequacies of contemporary life. They found this consolation in the Church, and in a literature which was as far removed as possible from the details of their actual surroundings: Lewis wrote science-fiction novels, Tolkien devised a mythology of his own creation, based on the models of Scandinavian legends. It seemed to him a virtue not to write 'realistically': 'The electric street-lamp may indeed be ignored simply because it is so insignificant and transient. Fairy-stories . . . have more permanent and fundamental things to talk about.'†

This distaste for the transient features of modern life is clear throughout *The Hobbit*, which reflects an England before the Industrial Revolution, before motorised transport or mechanical warfare. This is evident in the description of the goblins in Chapter 4: 'It is not unlikely that they invented some of the machines that have since troubled the world, especially the ingenious devices for killing large numbers of people at once . . . but in those days and those parts they had not advanced (as it is called) so far.' The permanent and fundamental things with which Tolkien was concerned were issues of man's relationship with his fellows, with the other creatures of the world, with the

*'On Fairy-stories' in *Tree and Leaf*, Allen & Unwin, London, 1964, p.36.'
†'On Fairy-stories', p.55.

earth itself, and with a system of values which controlled all of these and taught him what he could and could not do.

As a scholar, Tolkien was concerned with the earliest literature composed in English and the related literature of Scandinavia. The largest surviving English poem of this period, *Beowulf* (composed in the eighth century), had seemed to many earlier critics to be flawed as a work of literature because its central subject matter, the slaying of two monsters and a dragon, seemed of less interest than other themes which the poet merely touched upon. Tolkien's defence of the poem in his lecture 'Beowulf: The Monsters and the Critics' had much to say that is relevant to *The Hobbit*. His reading of the poem produced an interpretation in which the theme was 'man at war with the hostile world, and his inevitable overthrow in Time'.* The poem was written after the introduction of Christianity to England, but it describes an earlier, pagan world in which the dragon and the monsters could be identified with the powers of evil, and in which there is no mention of any Christian God. *The Hobbit* is also set in the past, and also lacks any explicit reference to a religion. But it does include a mythology, and Tolkien knew that mythology and religion could sometimes interact.† The system of values which operates in *The Hobbit* is derived from the ethics of the Old English poems that Tolkien taught, and also from his own Conservatism; but the system is also implicitly Christian, as is evident in Bilbo's reaction to Gollum:

> He must stab the foul thing, put its eyes out, kill it. It meant to kill him. No, not a fair fight. He was invisible now. Gollum had no sword. Gollum had not actually threatened to kill him, or tried to yet. And he was miserable, alone, lost. A sudden understanding, a pity mixed with horror, welled up in Bilbo's heart. (Chapter 5)

Part 3 of these Notes deals in some detail with the relationship between *The Hobbit* and *Beowulf*, with particular reference to the monsters of the two works, and what they represent.

Not all critics have reacted favourably to Tolkien's deliberate avoidance of natural, realistic settings. For some, as Joy Chant says, Tolkien's work has become 'a symbol . . . of an intellectual and emotional flaccidity in our society'.‡ It is only fair to point out that these critics were objecting not to the power of myth and legend, but to the fact that

*'Beowulf: The Monsters and the Critics' in *The Beowulf Poet*, edited by Donald K. Fry, Prentice-Hall, Englewood Cliffs, 1968, p.22.
†H. CARPENTER: *The Inklings*, Allen & Unwin, London, 1978, includes this quotation from one of the Inklings on p.226: 'We talked of Bishop Barnes . . . and how far pagan mythology was a substitute for theology.'
‡J. CHANT: 'Niggle and Numenor', *Children's Literature in Education*, APS Publications, New York, 1975, p.161.

Tolkien felt the need to invent a synthetic mythology. The writer of *Beowulf* could justifiably make use of the mythology of his ancestors, but some critics have seen less justification in Tolkien's creation of a mythology that has its origins in texts written so long ago that they can be read only with difficulty. Edmund Wilson, one of Tolkien's severest critics, was himself 'always interested in monsters'* but in the monsters from a real mythology, not an invented one. Ruth S. Noel, an admirer of Tolkien's work, makes an observation which could be taken as a criticism: 'Part of the puzzle arises from Tolkien's sharing a jest with his colleagues.'† If the reader is too much aware that Tolkien is sharing a joke with his colleagues, challenging them to spot the references to obscure literature, then Tolkien has failed as a writer, on his terms. He has failed to adhere to one of the rules laid down in the lecture 'On Fairy-stories': that everything inside the story must seem to be 'true'.

## Language and literature

Tolkien did not set out to write mythological fantasy. His composition of *The Silmarillion* developed out of an earlier interest in creating an artificial language. The work which occupied Tolkien's scholarly career, the study of the earliest phases of the history of the English language, involved a good deal of hypothesis and speculation about what the original forms of a particular word might have been. This led Tolkien to invent a language of his own, based upon the principles of organisation of Finnish, a language of which he had some knowledge. It was this invented language which led Tolkien to write fiction:

> I desired to do this for my own satisfaction, and I had little hope that other people would be interested in this work, especially since it was primarily linguistic in inspiration and was begun in order to provide the necessary background of 'history' for Elvish tongues.†

Tolkien knew that a language can only develop in response to the needs of its speakers, and will reflect their needs and their history. Tolkien could only develop his invented language thoroughly if he invented a history for its users. This was especially true of words which were the names of people or places. His Aunt Grace had told him when he was a boy that his own family name had a particular story attached to it:

> She alleged that the family name had originally been 'von Hohen-zollern'... A certain George von Hohenzollern had, she said, fought on the side of Archduke Ferdinand of Austria at the Siege of Vienna

---

*EDMUND WILSON: *The Twenties*, Macmillan, London, 1975, p.14.
†R.S. NOEL: *The Mythology of Middle-Earth*, Thames & Hudson, London, 1977, p.34.
‡*The Lord of the Rings*, Allen & Unwin, London, 1966, p.7.

in 1529. He had shown great daring in leading an unofficial raid against the Turks and capturing the Sultan's standard. This . . . was why he was given the nickname *Tolkkühn*, 'foolhardy'.*

Although this story was presumably untrue, it is sound in exemplifying one way in which English names can develop. Many an English surname reflects the life of one of the early members of the family: for example, the name Cooper indicates that the family had an ancestor who made barrels. Similarly, place-names do not spring from the air but derive from some physical feature, or commemorate a particular event in history (for example, Portsmouth, or Newcastle).

Tolkien took particular care over the names in *The Silmarillion*, such care that the work was never completed. *The Hobbit* reveals, on occasions, its author's fascination with the operations of language. A simple (and rather forced) example of this interest occurs in the opening chapter of the book in the reference to Old Took's great-granduncle Bullroarer:

> He charged the ranks of the goblins of Mount Gram in the Battle of the Green Fields, and knocked their king Golfimbul's head clean off with a wooden club. It sailed a hundred yards through the air and went down a rabbit-hole, and in this way the battle was won and the game of Golf invented at the same moment.

Tolkien is inventing an origin for the word 'golf' (which, in fact, is a word for which an origin has never been traced) by connecting it with the name of a goblin chieftain. This story is very close to the tale that he was told by his own Aunt Grace.

Throughout the book Tolkien is continually inventing names for people, places, and things, which are revealing of what they are, or how they came to be. The origins and meanings of these names are explained in Part 2 of these Notes, but it may be helpful here to examine the principles underlying these names.

Tolkien's fiction as a whole includes thirty-five different types of creatures (mortal, immortal, and monstrous) in addition to birds and animals, and he developed fifteen separate invented languages. Little of this complexity is evident in *The Hobbit*. The book contains no examples of creatures speaking in a language invented by Tolkien and even the names of places and things are straightforward in comparison to those in *The Lord of the Rings*. Place-names like the Lonely Mountain, River Running, and Dale are self-explanatory, as are the names of some of the characters in the book (for example, the Elvenking, the Master). It is a sign of the difference between *The Hobbit* and *The Lord of the Rings* that in *The Lord of the Rings* both the Elvenking and the Lonely

*H. CARPENTER: *J. R. R. Tolkien*, Allen & Unwin, London, 1977, pp.18–19.

Mountain receive new names which are much less easy to understand.

Many of the names in *The Hobbit* are taken from a single source: the Icelandic *Prose Edda* composed by Snorri Sturluson in the early thirteenth century. This work was encountered by Tolkien when he was a student and it provided him with the dwarf names in *The Hobbit* and with the name Gandalf for his wizard. Even the choice of Durin as the name for Thorin's ancestor was determined by the *Prose Edda* where a dwarf-prince called Durinn is one of the original ancestors of all the other dwarves.

Many of the names in *The Hobbit* are formed from English roots (like Hobbiton: the town of the Hobbits), or from obsolete English words no longer in use (like the name of the dragon, Smaug, which derives from an early English word meaning 'burrowing'); or, like the names of the dwarves, from a Scandinavian language. Some, however, are the product of Tolkien's own invention. The name Gondolin had a place in Tolkien's mythology as early as 1917 in his first attempt to write a tale from Elvish 'history'. The sound of this word, to an English ear, is much softer and more pleasant than the sound of the names which Tolkien gives his goblin leaders—Bolg and Azog. This establishes a principle that runs throughout his work: the evil characters are given harsh-sounding names, the good characters (especially the elves) have pleasant names.

One other principle of language is clearly illustrated in *The Hobbit*: different peoples can use different words to denote the same object or place, and the name given will often reflect the attitude of the people to that object. It is no accident that there are places in London bearing the names Trafalgar Square and Waterloo Bridge, whereas no French town commemorates these battles. In *The Hobbit* the swords found by the dwarves in the trolls' cave in Chapter 2 are known to the elves as the Goblin-cleaver and the Foe-hammer; to the goblins they are Biter and Beater. The names reflect very different attitudes to the swords on the part of the two races.

# The background to *The Hobbit*

It is tempting for any critic writing about *The Hobbit* to spend a good deal of time searching for parallels between Tolkien's fiction and the literature with which he was professionally concerned as a scholar and a teacher. However, rather than making particular comparisons between *The Hobbit* and the literature of medieval England, this section is concerned with Tolkien's attitude to that literature and the use he made of its system of values.

The literature which Tolkien spent his life lecturing on, and writing about, was written between about the middle of the seventh century and the early fourteenth century. It is conventional to describe the people of England before the twelfth century as the Anglo-Saxons and to call their language Old English. The literature of the Anglo-Saxons—and of their near-neighbours the Norsemen of Scandinavia—is among the earliest of northern Europe, and it might seem to describe, at first glance, a world so different from our own times as to be quite devoid of any relevance. Tolkien, however, felt that these ancient stories contained truths about man's place in the total context of history which were as valid now as when the stories were composed. Furthermore, he realised that the best of these early poems were not mere catalogues of battles but were, in fact, critical of those who gloried in warfare. They expressed the danger of a hero becoming too proud of his own achievements. Tolkien pointed out that a poem like *Beowulf* was written some time after the events which it was describing, and he saw the poem as an expression of man's inevitable downfall. It seemed to Tolkien that *Beowulf* was a lament, mourning the fact that nothing created by man is permanent, not even poetry itself. All must perish. The poem described a turning point in history, but the men involved in the story were not aware of the significance of the events which they were shaping.

In a similar fashion *The Hobbit* is set in the past, at a time when dragons were still prevalent. It is apparently the story of the reclaiming of Thorin's inheritance from the dragon, Smaug; but Tolkien himself decided later that its most significant episode was not the dispossession of the dragon, nor even his death, but Bilbo's discovery of the ring. To the dwarves and to Bilbo this discovery hardly seems momentous, yet it proves to be so significant that the lives of all the creatures on Earth are put into jeopardy, as Tolkien describes in *The Lord of the Rings*.

In the context of the total 'history' of the dwarves, elves, and hobbits, described in the whole of Tolkien's fiction, the death of Smaug is of no great import, and even within the scope of *The Hobbit* itself the adventure of Bilbo and the dwarves is not left entirely unquestioned. The quest of Thorin and his companions is increasingly suspect as the book goes on, and the dwarves are finally in great danger of becoming more like monsters than men. Tolkien creates a world in which quests for treasure are possible, only to leave the reader wondering if such quests are reasonable and just.

In this respect *The Hobbit* is remarkably similar to three of Tolkien's favourite works of medieval literature: *Beowulf*, *The Battle of Maldon*, and *Sir Gawain and the Green Knight*. In each of these three poems the reader has to undergo a change of heart: he is invited to admire the central figure in each of the poems, only to feel at the end that the hero may have behaved rashly and foolishly after all. In all three works the central figure acts in accordance with a set of principles accepted by those around him. In each case his action is shown to have been ultimately futile, and the writers in their different ways each imply that the social systems described in their work are flawed. In each case the writer is describing an earlier time, a world very different from that in which he lives.

## The heroic code

It is necessary to explain in a little more detail some of the features of the social code that dominates the literature of the Anglo-Saxons, and which underlies the behaviour of many of the characters in *The Hobbit*. The most objective summary of this code is to be found not in an English writer, but in the work of the Latin historian Tacitus (56–115), who wrote a description of the peoples of northern Europe. entitled *Germania*. His purpose was to emphasise the degeneracy of his own Roman society by contrasting it with the inherent civilisation of the less sophisticated northerners. Tacitus, like Tolkien, believed that change did not always lead to improvement; the old and simpler life may have its advantages. From Tacitus we learn of the code of honour and loyalty that bound together the people of such societies as the Anglo-Saxons. Theirs was a system in which every man owed allegiance to one or other chief, to whom he promised loyalty and from whom he received protection and reward. Tacitus saw how family groupings and military groupings tended to coincide: 'squadrons . . . are not made at random . . . but are each composed of men of one family or clan'* and he wrote of family ties which were particularly close: 'The sons of sisters are as highly honoured by their uncles as by their own fathers.'† It is easy to see how Tolkien has employed the same set of allegiances in describing the dwarves in *The Hobbit*. They too fight together in family units, and the bond between Fili and Kili and their uncle is so close that all three are buried together.

In the final battle, in Chapter 17 of *The Hobbit*, the forces of right unite behind Thorin in the struggle against the goblins. More surprisingly perhaps, a few chapters earlier, the dwarves are ready to follow Thorin even though they know him to be wrong: 'So grim had Thorin become, that even if they had wished, the others would not have dared to find fault with him' (Chapter 15). It is not merely Thorin's grimness which prevents any disagreement: the heroic code also demanded total obedience. As Tacitus says 'The chief fights for victory, the followers for their chief.'‡ It was considered shameful for soldiers to retreat from the battle if their lord was slain. They either fought on to victory, or

* *The Agricola and the Germania*, translated by H. Mattingly, Penguin Books, Harmondsworth, 1948, Section 7.
† Section 20.
‡ Section 14.

died alongside their leader. Thus an irresponsible leader could doom a whole army to destruction. In Part 3 of these Notes there is a detailed discussion of the way in which Tolkien employs this system in his portrayal of various kinds of leaders in *The Hobbit*.

In Anglo-Saxon society a lord who was successful in battle would be generous to his followers, sharing with them the spoils of war. Tolkien makes use of this system of service and reward, but he sets it alongside a more modern system of trade and agriculture, and there are some characters in the book who feel that the old ways are no longer valid.

The worst possible fate for any man in Anglo-Saxon society was to lose his position within the lord's hall. A man with no lord to protect him had no status and, indeed, exile was considered an even greater punishment than death. There are two characters in *The Hobbit* whose presentation is affected by Tolkien's awareness of the plight of the exile. Gollum evokes pity in his pathetic isolation. He is accepted by nobody. In contrast, Bilbo Baggins, who might have had a similar fate as the only hobbit on the quest, is able to demonstrate that solitude is not necessarily intolerable. Because of his strength of character he turns solitude to his advantage and finally wins the respect of a whole range of creatures.

## A note on the text

There are now so many published versions of *The Hobbit* that it is impossible to estimate which edition is most likely to be in the possession of any particular reader. The references in these Notes are to the English edition published by Allen and Unwin, London, 1972, with an introduction by R.S. Fowler.* It incorporates the revisions made by Tolkien between the first edition of 1937 and the second of 1951. The references in this text are always to chapters rather than to pages, so the reader should have no difficulty, whatever edition is used. References to *The Lord of the Rings* are cited by Book, Chapter, and (where necessary) Appendix.

---

*J.R.R. TOLKIEN, *The Hobbit*, introduced by R.S. Fowler, Allen & Unwin, London, 1972.

# Part 2

# Summaries
## *of* THE HOBBIT

## A general summary

Bilbo Baggins, a hobbit leading a quiet and unexciting life, finds himself involved in an adventure with thirteen dwarves and a wizard called Gandalf. They are to travel eastward to the Lonely Mountain in order to reclaim from Smaug, the dragon, treasure which was taken from the dwarves' ancestors. They first encounter three trolls who put the dwarves into sacks. Gandalf is able to set the trolls fighting among themselves and keep them arguing until the day breaks and the trolls are turned to stone. The dwarves are released and they find swords and treasure hidden in the trolls' cave.

After a short rest in Rivendell, home of the elves, the travellers climb the Misty Mountains where they are forced to seek shelter in a cave in order to escape from a fierce storm. The cave proves to be part of the goblins' underground territory, and the dwarves are captured once again. This time Gandalf uses his power over fire to release them but, as they rush away from the goblins, the dwarves lose Bilbo who, in the darkness, comes across a ring. Alone underground he meets a creature in a lake, and each tries to establish the strengths and weaknesses of the other. They test each other through a riddle game and Bilbo wins. The creature, Gollum, is furious at Bilbo and it is only by using the ring (which, as Bilbo discovers, makes the wearer invisible) that the hobbit is able to escape from Gollum and the goblins.

Having emerged from the mountains, Bilbo is reunited with the dwarves and they set off eastward once more. They are beset by wolves and then by goblins and are saved in the nick of time by a flock of eagles who carry them up to their eyries. On the following morning the eagles set them on their way again. The travellers find an unusual ally in Beorn—a creature who can change from a man into a bear—who gives them not only food and shelter, but also provisions for their journey. As they enter Mirkwood Gandalf finally leaves the party, warning them not to drink the water or to stray from the path. Nevertheless, when their provisions have run out, the dwarves succumb to the lure of elvish lights in the forest and find themselves hopelessly lost in Mirkwood. Bilbo eventually finds his friends in the power of huge spiders, but with the help of his magic ring and a great deal of courage, he releases them.

Only when the fight is over do they realise that Thorin, the leader of the dwarves, is missing. He has been captured by elves and taken to the palace of the Elvenking on the edge of Mirkwood. Soon he is joined in the dungeons by the other dwarves, also captured by elves. Only Bilbo is free, and he organises an escape, taking messages from dwarf to dwarf and finally hitting on the plan of getting the dwarves out of the palace by hiding them in empty barrels and floating them downstream. After a rough passage the dwarves emerge from their barrels at Esgaroth, the Lake-town, where Thorin is welcomed as 'The King under the Mountain' who has returned to rid them of the dragon, Smaug.

Although Bilbo and the dwarves are given ponies and provisions by the men of Lake-town, they are left to tackle Smaug without any further help. Bilbo eventually finds the secret door in the west of the mountain, and he enters Smaug's cave. He steals a cup from the dragon's hoard, which infuriates the beast. On his second visit to Smaug, however, Bilbo discovers that Smaug has a weak spot, and when the enraged dragon sets off to vent his fury on the men of the Lake-town, Bilbo and the dwarves raid his lair and then leave the Lonely Mountain for a safer place.

Smaug destroys the Lake-town but is himself killed by a man called Bard who is told by a bird of Smaug's weak spot. The Elvenking, on his way to the Lonely Mountain to seek the treasure for himself, helps Bard to make shelters for the people of the Lake-town. The elves and the men then join forces and march on the Lonely Mountain. By the time they arrive there they find that the Front Gate has already been fortified against attack because the dwarves have been warned by the birds of their approach. Thorin refuses to yield any of the treasure to Bard, even though Bilbo feels that his claim is just. Thorin sends to his cousin Dain to come to his aid. The dwarves are besieged in the Mountain and there seems to be no way of breaking the stalemate until Bilbo decides to take the Arkenstone—the most precious stone in the hoard, which Bilbo found earlier—and give it to Bard to use in his bargaining. When he takes it to the elves' camp he finds Gandalf there, who congratulates him on his cunning.

Thorin is angry when he discovers what Bilbo has done and he curses him and sends him to Bard. Dain arrives with his dwarves and it seems that a major battle is to take place, when a new enemy appears: goblins, accompanied by wolves. The elves, dwarves, and men fight together against this new foe, but it seem certain that they are to lose, until Beorn and the eagles suddenly appear and drive away the goblins.

Bilbo is knocked unconscious in the fray and when he comes to, the battle is over. Thorin has been mortally wounded but his dying words are of friendship to Bilbo. After the funeral of Thorin (and of Fili and Kili who died with him) Bilbo bids farewell to the dwarves and sets off home with Gandalf. They spend the winter with Beorn and with Elrond in Rivendell before arriving at Hobbiton, where Bilbo has been given up for dead and his property is being sold. He is able to recover most of his goods and settles down happily to writing his memoirs. One day Gandalf visits him with Balin, the friendliest of all the dwarves, and they talk of times past, and of the peace that has come to those who live around the Lonely Mountain.

# Detailed summaries

## Chapter 1: An Unexpected Party

This introduces us to Bilbo Baggins, a hobbit leading a comfortable and quiet life despite the fact that his mother had the reputation of being rather remarkable. He is visited one April morning by someone he does not at first recognise, who is looking for a companion on an adventure. Bilbo is rather patronising until this stranger reveals himself as Gandalf, a wizard whose fame excites the hobbit. Rather against his will Bilbo finds that he has invited the wizard for tea.

On the following day thirteen dwarves arrive for tea, one after the other: Dwalin, Balin, Kili, Fili, Dori, Nori, Ori, Oin, Gloin, Bifur, Bofur, Bombur, and Thorin. Bilbo is puzzled at their arrival and irritated at having to feed them as well as Gandalf. The dwarves, however, help him to wash and clean the dishes, and in the evening Bilbo finds himself enchanted by their songs which make him dream of adventure.

Thorin Oakenshield, leader of the dwarves, reveals that they have been lured to Bilbo's home by a secret mark which Gandalf put on the door and which meant 'Burglar wants a good job, plenty of excitement and reasonable reward'. The dwarves are about to embark on an adventure and were led to believe by Gandalf's sign that Bilbo might be the extra companion they needed.

Bilbo faints at the first thought of a dangerous journey, and the dwarves are sceptical about whether Gandalf has chosen wisely. Gandalf, however, insists that Bilbo has hidden qualities, and the hobbit himself (when he regains consciousness) maintains that he is indeed brave, though not a burglar and quite unaware of the mark on the door.

Gandalf reveals the details of the adventure. He unrolls a map of the destination and talks of a dragon and a small, secret door, through which a burglar is to gain entry. Eventually Bilbo is told the full story from the beginning: the Mountain lies away to the east and was, in times gone by, the home of Thorin's ancestors. It was transformed by the dwarves into a vast palace full of gold and jewels, and at that time they lived in peace with the men who lived in the nearby town of Dale. The fame of the dwarves' treasure reached the dragon, Smaug, who laid waste the land around the Mountain, killing dwarves, destroying Dale, and taking over the treasure as his own. Some dwarves survived, but they were forced to leave the land around the Mountain and to take whatever work they could find: but always they planned to return and to depose the dragon.

Gandalf now reveals that he met Thorin's imprisoned father, Thrain, and was given the map which they have been studying, and also a key to the secret door in the side of the Mountain. He persuades Thorin not to seek revenge on his father's murderer, the Necromancer, but instead to go back to the Mountain. Bilbo finds himself agreeing to go on the adventure, and they all go to bed, but not before ordering their breakfasts from the hobbit.

NOTES AND GLOSSARY:

| | |
|---|---|
| **hobbit:** | the origins of this word are explained on p.49 |
| **panelled walls:** | wooden wall-covering, found in old, grand houses in England |
| **pantries:** | small rooms for storing food: already preparing us for the preoccupation with eating which is to be a characteristic of Bilbo throughout the novel |
| **well-to-do:** | affluent |
| **Belladonna Took:** | Belladonna means 'beautiful lady'. It is also the name of a poison |
| **Gandalf:** | for the origin of this name, and the names of all the dwarves, see p.11 |
| **Good Morning:** | this conventional greeting is examined critically by Gandalf and this makes Bilbo rather irritated |
| **magic diamond studs:** | in the days before shirts were mass-produced they were fastened by studs rather than by buttons |
| **unexpected luck of widows' sons:** | many legends centre on characters who are initially extremely unfortunate (as in having no father to earn a living for the family), thus increasing the reader's pleasure at their later success. *Jack and the Beanstalk* and *Aladdin* are examples |
| **Midsummer's Eve:** | a time of the year when magic might be expected, as in Shakespeare's *A Midsummer Night's Dream* |
| **Going off into the Blue:** | going away with no definite destination in mind |
| **quite inter-:** | Bilbo is about to say 'interesting', but stops himself |
| **I beg your pardon:** | a conventional expression of apology which Gandalf takes quite literally by granting his pardon to Bilbo. In this, and in his quibbling over 'Good Morning', Gandalf is challenging Bilbo's style of language and, by implication, his unadventurous way of life |

**Engagement Tablet:** a kind of diary in which Bilbo records his appointments: the capital letters make the name seem pompous and ridiculous

**a little stiff:** Bilbo's language is rather formal

**to go without:** as a good host Bilbo would have to ensure that his guests were fed. If there were too few cakes, then he would not have any

**after-supper morsel:** a delicate piece of paradox for comic effect: supper is normally the last meal of the day, so that there can be no such thing as an 'after-supper morsel'. Furthermore a morsel is a small portion of food, and this label can hardly be applied to two seed-cakes. Throughout this chapter Tolkien is ridiculing the excessive amount of food consumed by Bilbo

**throng:** a large gathering of people

**porter:** a strong variety of beer, very dark in colour

**thirteen hoods:** thirteen is considered an unlucky number, and one of the reasons why the dwarves are anxious to have another companion on their journey is to avoid the ill-luck that might befall a party of thirteen

**flummoxed:** confused

**confusticate and bebother these dwarves:** Bilbo's own oaths calling down curses on the dwarves

**the crocks:** the crockery: plates and dishes

**the fender:** a guard rail placed around a fire to prevent people from getting too close to it

**fiddles:** violins

**ere:** before

**yore:** times gone by

**the fells:** the hills

**elvish lord:** lord of the elves. Tolkien uses 'elvish' and 'elven' as adjectives derived from 'elf'

**wrought:** created, fashioned

**goblets:** large, ornate drinking-vessels

**delves:** digs. The song is written in a kind of language which is removed from everyday English, including outmoded, archaic forms like 'delves' and 'yore'. The subject it describes is similar to early English poems of buried treasure (see p.58)

**dragon's ire:** dragon's anger

**something Tookish:** something which derived from the more adventurous side of Bilbo's ancestry, from his mother, Belladonna Took

**less than half a mind:** the expression 'to have half a mind to do something' indicates an incomplete commitment to a task. Bilbo has less than half a mind, and so his resolve is very uncertain. Fear is uppermost in his feelings

**audacious:** daring, bold

**estimable:** worthy of esteem and respect

**in a pinch:** in a dangerous situation

**and the game of Golf . . . moment:** a rather laboured attempt at a joke. (See p.10)

**drawing-room:** a room in a house, often kept unused except for special occasions and visitors

**parlour:** the room used for everyday living

**put your foot in it:** got into trouble

**being on his dignity:** speaking in a way intended to show that his feelings had been hurt

**were-worms:** a word which Tolkien has invented on the pattern of 'werewolf'. A werewolf is a creature which changes from man to wolf at different times, and so a 'were-worm' would be a creature which changed from a man into a dragon

**digging coal:** the dwarves are associated with mining and tunnelling, and the most degrading form of this activity which Gandalf can image is to dig coal. (See p.54)

**a lot more than you can guess . . . himself:** these prophetic words are to be proved true in the course of the novel

**I remember the Mountain:** the reader is not intended to be able to follow this section. The story is to be told fully and in chronological order later in the chapter

**the Mountain:** later referred to in this book as the Lonely Mountain

**Mirkwood:** the name of the forest is based upon the word 'murky' which means dark, and threatening

**the Withered Heath:** in the Welsh collection of tales, *The Mabinogion*, there is a story of a dragon who destroys all the crops of the land for seven miles around his lair

**runes:** letters from an alphabet used in Europe from about the second century. They were believed to have magical properties

**you will see there the runes in red:** some later editions of the novel do not have the runes in colour

**dragons are comfortably . . . legendary:** Tolkien is suggesting here, through Gandalf, that our own scepticism about the existence of dragons may be simply a result of the fact that they live far away from us

**the mortal men:** human beings

**armour and jewels and carvings and cups:** the kinds of treasure described here are exactly those made by the craftsmen of the Anglo-Saxons in early England

**worm:** dragon

**sinking as low . . . coalmining:** see the note above on **digging coal**

**Moria . . . Azog the Goblin:** this reference prepares us for the hatred between dwarves and goblins which we are to find later in the novel

**the Necromancer:** a 'Necromancer' is a kind of magician who attempts to communicate with the dead. This particular Necromancer plays only a minor role in this novel, not even being given a name. He is treated here and at the end of the book (see Chapter 19) as the most dangerous of all enemies, who will continue to exert evil even when such minor sources of badness as Smaug have been destroyed. In *The Lord of the Rings* Tolkien describes this threat in much greater detail, and names him Sauron

**hear hear:** an expression signifying agreement: taken literally by the dwarves

---

## Chapter 2: Roast Mutton

---

Bilbo wakes the next morning to find that all the dwarves have gone, leaving only a pile of unwashed plates behind. He washes these and eats a leisurely breakfast. Gandalf appears and reprimands him, drawing his attention to a message left by the dwarves on the mantelpiece. The note is addressed to Burglar Bilbo and offers him a fourteenth share of the profits of the expedition in exchange for his assistance.

Bilbo has just ten minutes to make the appointment with the dwarves at the Green Inn, Bywater, and sets off at a run without even a hat or a handkerchief. The dwarves are waiting with ponies and baggage already laden and, borrowing a hood and a cloak from Dwalin, Bilbo sets off with them.

In the company of Gandalf they travel eastward for many days, gradually leaving familiar country. Suddenly, one wet and miserable day, Gandalf leaves them, and they are unable even to get their fire alight. There seems to be a fire in the woods ahead of them and Bilbo is sent off to investigate. He discovers three trolls eating their supper in a clearing and foolishly tries to steal a purse from them. He is caught, but is able to escape out of the firelight while the trolls are arguing over his fate. The dwarves, however, have followed Bilbo into the wood and one by one they are all captured except Thorin, and are put into sacks.

Thorin is warned by Bilbo as he approaches the clearing and the two start to fight the trolls. Gandalf arrives just as they have both been overpowered; he is able to rescue all of them by setting the trolls arguing and keeping the quarrel going until dawn, when the trolls are turned to stone by the first rays of the light. After the dwarves are released they search for the trolls' cave but are unable to gain entry until Bilbo produces a key which has fallen from the pocket of one of the trolls.

Inside the cave they find swords, and a knife which serves as a weapon for Bilbo. After a meal the party hides some of the treasure in case they can return to claim it one day. Gandalf reveals that he has been ahead to Rivendell to arrange for their provisions to be restocked, and this is their next destination.

NOTES AND GLOSSARY:

**outlandish:** ridiculous, impossible to believe

**nice little second breakfast:** Bilbo's greed again

**Great Elephants:** Gandalf's own oath, expressing his incredulity

**paraphernalia:** miscellaneous goods

**Bother burgling:** an oath invoking a curse on burglary

**the kettle just beginning to sing:** a kettle 'sings' as the steam rises just before it starts to boil

**mighty little:** very little

**canny:** well-ordered

**toothsome:** rousing to the appetite

**trolls:** the word 'troll' is found in Scandinavian mythology, denoting a race of giants living in caves

**which was not drawing-room fashion:** Bilbo's own language is modelled on a polite variety of spoken English (marked, for example, by very mild oaths like 'bother', and by the restraint he displays in the opening chapter even when visited by fourteen strangers). On the other hand, Tolkien gives the trolls a language based upon working-class London speech

**blimey:** a working-class oath (originally meaning 'May I be blinded if I do not speak the truth')

**tomorrer:** tomorrow (Tolkien is attempting to describe features of pronunciation in his spelling of the trolls' speech)

**a blinking bit:** 'blinking' is a meaningless adjective often used for emphasis by lower-class users of English

**what the 'ell:** 'What the Hell' is an oath meaning 'What on earth'. It is characteristic of careless speakers of English to omit the initial sound 'h' and also the final 'g' from words ending in 'ing'

**yer:** your (sometimes 'you')

**et:** eaten

**wiped his lips on his sleeve:** the trolls speak in a debased way and their general behaviour is consistent with this: they argue, drink from a jug, and do not use handkerchiefs

**even those ... head each:** the implication is that these trolls are closer to human beings than most because they have only one head each. Presumably other multi-headed trolls behave in an even worse manner

**pinched:**
**purloined:** } stolen

**warming to:** becoming enthusiastic about

**are the mischief:** are the most deceitful of things

**'oo:** who

**copped:** caught; found

**lumme:** an expression of surprise

**a bur- a hobbit:** Bilbo is about to confess to being a burglar, but checks himself in time. The trolls think he has described himself as a 'burrahobbit'

**throttled:** strangled

**in the uptake:** in understanding

**and cook better than I cook:** I am better at preparing food than I am at being eaten

**blighter:** fellow

**a gorgeous row:** an immense quarrel

**all sorts of perfectly true and applicable names:** almost all of the curses in English have some other quite literal meaning, often referring to a part of the anatomy or to some sexual practice. Tolkien is suggesting that the curses of the trolls were appropriate in a literal sense

**trolls simply detest ... (uncooked):** trolls would be very pleased to see cooked dwarves

**a nice pickle:** a fine mess

**booby:** fool

**dawn take you all, and be stone to you:** May the dawn take you and turn you all to stone. It is traditional that trolls turn to stone when exposed to daylight

**spells:** magic incantations

---

## Chapter 3: A Short Rest

---

The party continue on their journey until they come within sight of the Misty Mountains. They are met by elves who lead them to the valley of

Rivendell and the house of Elrond. They stay there for over two weeks, eating, resting, and refreshing themselves. Elrond explains that the swords which the dwarves took from the trolls were made by elves to slay goblins, and that they carry the names Orcrist and Glamdring. Elrond also finds moon letters on the dwarves' map which reveal that on Durin's Day the last light of the setting sun will reveal the keyhole in the secret door. The following morning the travellers set off again on their journey.

NOTES AND GLOSSARY:

| | |
|---|---|
| **be done for:** | be destroyed |
| **homely:** | welcoming |
| **pretty well:** | fairly well (understatement) |
| **faggots:** | bundles of twigs |
| **bannocks:** | flat oat-cakes |
| **jolly:** | pleasant, full of happiness |
| **delicious:** | amusing |
| **palpitating:** | terrifying |
| **gruesome:** | gory; involving loss of blood |
| **he comes into many tales:** | this assertion gives the impression that Tolkien is reciting a genuine piece of mythology, and has a choice of tales open to him from which he has opted to tell of Thorin and Smaug |
| **very old swords:** | Elrond, like a warrior in an early English poem, has a reverence for old weapons that have proved their worth |
| **Gondolin:** | Tolkien gives the history of this city in *The Silmarillion* |
| **Orcrist . . . Glamdring:** | it was a common practice to give names to swords in order to increase their potency. Beowulf, for example, uses a sword called Hrunting to defeat Grendel's mother |
| **Durin's Day:** | there would not necessarily be a day every year when both sun and moon were visible in the sky at once |

## Chapter 4: Over Hill and Under Hill

The party rides up into the Misty Mountains for many days until one day a terrible thunderstorm forces them to take shelter in a cave which Fili and Kili claim to have thoroughly explored. All of the party fall asleep except Bilbo, who sees to his horror that the floor of the cave is gradually slipping away and that the ponies have already disappeared through a crack in the wall. As he shouts out a number of goblins appear and the dwarves are captured, although Gandalf is able to escape.

Bilbo and the dwarves are taken deep into the inside of the mountain where the ponies are being herded together ready for the goblins to eat. After questioning the dwarves, the goblin chief becomes very angry when he sees their swords. He is about to seize Thorin when all the lights go out and a terrifying pillar of smoke sends out sparks to attack the goblins.

Gandalf, who produced the pillar, leads the dwarves out of danger, with Dori carrying Bilbo on his back. The light from the elvish swords increases in the presence of goblins and frightens them away. Eventually, however, the goblins catch them from behind and Bilbo is knocked unconscious.

NOTES AND GLOSSARY:

**haymaking . . . blackberrying:** Bilbo traces the journey in terms of a natural cycle of agriculture. Haymaking would take place in May, and he expects that it will be late August (blackberrying) before they have crossed the mountains

**and that was the last time . . . with them:** here Tolkien gives us a warning that something disastrous is to happen

**knew their way, as well as you do to the nearest post-office:** knew their way as well as you do to the most familiar of local buildings

**Clap! Snap!:** the song of the goblins is notable for the harshness of its sounds

**yammer:** babble

**quaff:** drink

**whooped:** shouted

**eat horses . . . more dreadful things:** in England, unlike many other countries, horse meat is not normally eaten

**they had not advanced (as it called):** the use of the parenthesis indicates that Tolkien does not consider that the development of bombs is a sign of advancement

**I'll warrant:** I am sure

**went off poof!:** expressive of the sound of the fire being extinguished

**skriking:** screaming

---

## Chapter 5: Riddles in the Dark

---

When Bilbo opens his eyes again he is alone in the dark. As he feels his way along the ground his hand touches a ring which he puts into his pocket. His dagger glows in the dark, thus proving itself to be an elvish blade made to slay goblins. He walks along until he finds himself by the side of the waters of a lake. Unfortunately he cannot get across it because he has never learned to swim.

In the lake lives a hideous man-like creature called Gollum who comes across to Bilbo's side before the hobbit is even aware of his presence. The two become involved in a riddle-game while each tries to work out the strengths and weaknesses of the other. The rules of the game are that if Bilbo fails to answer he will be eaten; but if he sets a riddle which Gollum cannot answer, then Gollum will do anything he wishes.

This game continues for some time with neither able to gain an advantage, until Gollum asks Bilbo to pose a question for him to answer. Bilbo claims, as his prize, that Gollum show him the way out of the mountain, but Gollum only feigns agreement. He returns to his island intending to find his most treasured possession, a magic ring that renders the wearer invisible. Gollum plans to use the ring to overpower Bilbo, but realises that he has lost it.

Bilbo hears Gollum's screams of anguish and starts to run away from the lake. As Gollum gains on him he slips the ring in his pocket on to his finger and is astonished to find that Gollum rushes past him, apparently unable to see him. Thus Bilbo finds himself following Gollum, who talks to himself as he runs and thereby reveals to Bilbo the nature of the ring's power. Eventually Gollum leads Bilbo to a passage which will bring him out of the mountain. With a great leap, Bilbo jumps over Gollum and heads for freedom.

The exit from the passage is guarded by armed goblins who rush at Bilbo, because he has allowed the ring to slip from his finger. He quickly regains his invisibility, however, and scrambles to the door. Even though he gets stuck in the door and his shadow is seen by one of the guards, he is nevertheless able to squeeze out. Keeping out of the sunlight, he runs down the side of the mountain.

NOTES AND GLOSSARY:

**it was a turning point in his career:** again we are given advance warning of what is to be a significant element in the tale

**miserabler:** the normal form would be 'more miserable'

**that was something:** that was quite important

**breeches:** trousers

**only one thing to do:** this speech shows Bilbo's determination and bravery

**a tight place:** a dangerous situation

**so it is a pool:** Bilbo is able to reach this conclusion from the fact that he cannot hear the sound of a current

**unbeknown:**     unknown
**Gollum:**     as this chapter explains, the name comes from the sound which the creature makes in his throat. When Tolkien re-tells this story in *The Lord of the Rings* he includes the earlier history of Gollum when he lived above ground and was called Smeagol
**bless us and splash us:** Gollum consistently refers to himself in the plural. This oath is quite appropriate to Gollum
**precioussss:**     the spelling is meant to suggest the way in which Gollum dwells on the last sound of the word
**praps:**     perhaps
**a bitsy:**     a little bit
**Thirty white houses . . . stand still:** this is a traditional riddle of great venerability. Riddles are among the earliest forms of literature in English. *The Exeter Book*, a manuscript collection of Old English poems, includes some ninety-five riddles
**chestnuts:**     an expression applied to sayings or jokes which are extremely well-known
**eggses:**     eggs
**till it tired him . . . galled him:** this hint that the ring might have an effect over the mind and well-being of its wearer is fully developed in *The Lord of the Rings*
**noser:**     inquisitive person (a word of Gollum's invention)
**brought Bilbo's heart to his mouth:** made Bilbo feel terrified
**orcs:**     large goblins
**to-do:**     commotion

---

## Chapter 6: Out of the Frying-Pan into the Fire

Bilbo finds that he has gone right through the Misty Mountains and is now alone on the other side. As he wanders down the mountainside he hears voices ahead of him and realises that it is Gandalf and the dwarves. By using his ring Bilbo is able to slip past Balin, who is on guard, and step unseen into the midst of the dwarves. This enhances Bilbo's reputation for stealth, and he tells them nothing of the ring although he relates the rest of his adventure with Gollum. He learns that Gandalf had followed the goblins and used his magical powers to summon fire and to free the dwarves.

Although the company have had neither rest nor food, Gandalf urges them on in order to get as far away from the goblins as possible. They reach a clearing on their march, but are forced to climb into the trees when they hear the sound of wolves. Bilbo has difficulty in climbing and just manages to get into a tree when the Wargs arrive.

Gandalf understands the language of the Wargs and learns that they are in league with the goblins, and have planned to meet them in the clearing on this very night. The plan had been for the Wargs and the goblins to join in an attack upon a nearby village. Now, however, the Wargs are puzzled that the goblins have failed to arrive. In order to drive off the Wargs Gandalf sets light to some of the pine cones and throws them down on the Wargs, who run away in terror.

It appears that this victory will be short-lived for the goblins arrive and put out all the fires except those which are burning around the trees in which the company are hiding. The goblins sing a song of triumph as the fire gets closer to the trees. The Lord of the Eagles, who has been circling overhead watching the events of the night, swoops with a flock of his birds, and carries Bilbo, Gandalf, and the dwarves off to a high eyrie.

Bilbo is at first terrified that the eagles mean to harm them, but all is well. The Lord of the Eagles agrees to set the travellers down on the ground far away from the goblins. The party spend the night on a rock shelf, eating a supper of rabbits, hares, and a small sheep.

NOTES AND GLOSSARY:

**dells:** valleys

**drat him:** ⎫
**confusticate him:** ⎭ may he be damned

**I take off my hood to you:** the conventional expression of admiration is 'I take off my hat to you'. The baring of one's head is an indication of respect

**everything—except about ... the ring:** In *The Lord of the Rings* a major theme is the way in which those who wear the ring become corrupted by it. There is a hint of that theme in Bilbo's furtiveness here

**benighted:** lost at night

**more or less decent:** reasonably respectable

**very ticklish:** very dangerous

**touch and go:** close to going wrong

**blackberries were still ... flower:** a further reference to the passing of the year in terms of the cycle of nature. (See p.25)

**gone cracked:** gone mad

**a decent fellow:** a good-hearted fellow

**Wargs:** from the Icelandic word for wolf, 'varg'

**has not happened for a long while:** Tolkien attempts to make the story more real by this hint that goblins might once again march to war

**yammering:** howling

**bracken:** a kind of fern

| | |
|---|---|
| **pine-needles:** | the leaves of the pine tree |
| **reek:** | foul smell |
| **bird-nesting time:** | the time when small boys take the eggs from birds' nests |
| **fizzling:** | burning noisily |
| **'em:** | them |
| **turn queer:** | become dizzy |
| **yew:** | the wood of the yew tree, especially renowned for its strength |
| **boughs:** | branches |
| **tinder-boxes:** | a method of creating sparks to light a fire |

## Chapter 7: Queer Lodgings

Early the next morning the travellers resume their journey. They are set down by the eagles on the ground close to a stream. Hardly have they landed when Gandalf announces that he will soon be leaving them; but he promises to stay until they have found food and transport, and he hints that there is someone in the area who might help.

Gandalf explains that Beorn might be willing to help them and describes him as a quick-tempered man, who has the ability to change his shape. The trip to Beorn's house fascinates the travellers as the terrain starts to change and they see huge honey-bees.

Because Beorn would be suspicious of a large number of visitors, Gandalf has to employ a ruse to get all of the party into his house. He arrives at the door accompanied only by Bilbo and gradually interests Beorn in the story of their adventures so far, introducing the dwarves in pairs as the tale goes on. Beorn is so intrigued by the story that he scarcely notices that his house has been filled by fifteen strangers, and he is so delighted at the entertaining tale that he invites them all to stay for supper.

At supper the travellers are waited upon by Beorn's animals: horses, dogs, sheep, and ponies. They enjoy the meal, and the dwarves fall to telling tales. Eventually Beorn leaves them, but not without having prepared beds for each of the party. Throughout the following day there is no sign of either Beorn or Gandalf, but the wizard finally returns at supper-time and tells them that he has been following bear-tracks. A great meeting of bears has been held during the night and, from the tracks, Gandalf knows that they have gone towards the Misty Mountains. Bilbo is afraid that Beorn might have betrayed the travellers and will bring the goblins back to kill them, but his fears prove groundless when Beorn returns in the morning. He explains that he has been verifying Gandalf's story, and has killed a goblin and a Warg.

Beorn offers to help Bilbo and the dwarves by providing them with ponies (and a horse for Gandalf) as well as with food. He asks them to send back the ponies and the horse when they reach the edge of the forest, and he delivers a stern warning against drinking any of the water that they may find in Mirkwood.

The party reach the edge of Mirkwood, having been followed on the way by what Bilbo thinks is a bear. Gandalf reminds them that they must return their ponies, and reveals that Beorn himself has been tracking them in the guise of a bear. It is at this moment that Gandalf bids farewell to the travellers, with a final warning not to stray from the path. The company shoulder their packs and march into the forest.

NOTES AND GLOSSARY:

**and though the Lord ... Five Armies:** Tolkien prepares for future events here in two ways: by alluding to a gift which the goblins are to make in the future to the eagles, and by the reference to the battle

**a wholesome one:** in contrast to the cave in the Misty Mountain which looked welcoming but proved treacherous, this cave really does provide shelter

**plight:** difficulty

**Carrock:** a word derived from Old English 'carr' meaning stone, plus 'rock'

**Beorn:** the Old English word 'beorn' means 'man' as well as 'hero'. It is connected with the Scandinavian word for bear

**rug, cape ... word:** all of the words in this list are the names of the products of animal skins, and since Beorn is part animal it would be unfortunate to use such words in his presence

**hornets:** insects, of the wasp family

**drones:** male bees. On the significance of bees to Beorn, see p.55

**tunic:** a loose garment

**laughed a great rolling laugh ... axe:** Beorn's axe, his huge laugh, and his ability to change his shape, all link him with the Green Knight in the medieval romance *Sir Gawain and the Green Knight*

**veranda:** a room built on to the exterior of a house, with a roof but without solid walls; used in the summer

**westering:** setting in the west

**jack-in-the-boxes:** a jack-in-the-box is a toy which consists of a puppet on a spring in a box. When the lid of the box is opened the spring pushes the puppet out very suddenly

**frightfully polite:**    extremely polite
**mead:**    an alcoholic drink, made of fermented honey
**a regular bears' meeting:** a true bears' meeting
**felt quite crushed:**  felt that what he had said was regarded as foolish
**it carries enchantment:** there are many literary precedents for streams which carry waters of forgetfulness. John Milton (1608–74), for example, includes one in his description of Hell in the epic *Paradise Lost* (1667)
**steeds:**    ponies and horses
**it is a thousand to one:** there is very little chance at all

---

## Chapter 8: Flies and Spiders

---

The company march through the dark and hateful forest. When they make camp at night, sinister insect eyes surround them and their fire attracts huge moths and bats.

After several days their provisions are running low and there is no way of replenishing them in the forest. They remember Beorn's warning and, despite their thirst, they do not drink from the Mirkwood stream. Eventually they need to cross the water, and fortunately Bilbo sees a boat on the opposite bank. Fili is able to get a rope on the boat and the dwarves pull it across to their side of the stream.

Almost all of the company have crossed in safety when a deer darts from the forest. Thorin's attempt to shoot it distracts the dwarves' attention from the fact that Bombur has fallen in the stream. He is pulled out, but he has sunk into a deep sleep, and the boat has floated away.

The dwarves stand and curse their ill luck when more deer appear on the path ahead of them. Impetuously the dwarves shoot all their arrows at the deer, in vain. Thus they journey on, taking it in turn to carry the sleeping Bombur. After several more weary days Thorin calls for a volunteer to climb up a tall tree to determine the extent of the forest. Because he is the lightest and will not bend the more slender branches, Bilbo is chosen; but he is unable to see any end to the trees. This infuriates the dwarves, who pay no attention to Bilbo's description of the beautiful butterflies he has seen.

That night the company eat their last scraps of food, comforted only by the fact that Bombur suddenly wakes again. He is able to remember nothing of their journey and weeps to find that they have no food. They march on miserably for another day until Bombur refuses to go any further. Just at that moment Balin sees a light in the forest and the members of the company, remembering Gandalf's instruction not to leave the path, argue whether they should investigate the light. They decide to send out two spies, but nobody is willing to volunteer; so, urged on by Bombur's descriptions of the feasts he has been dreaming of, they all plunge into the forest.

They are led by the light into a clearing where elvish folk are holding a feast—but as they rush forward to beg for food, all the lights and fires go out and the dwarves are left alone. They prepare to spend the night in the clearing, but after a short while they are roused by Dori, who has seen more lights in a different part of the forest.

Again they are led to a feast and again the lights are extinguished as they approach. This time they almost lose Bilbo in the darkness. Again they settle down for this night in this second clearing, and are roused this time by Kili. For a third time the lights of the feast go out as soon as they attempt to enter the clearing; and worse still, Bilbo becomes separated from the rest of the company.

As he sits by a tree waiting for day to break, Bilbo's legs are wrapped in sticky, string-like fibres. Suddenly a great spider rushes at him. Bilbo is able to defend himself with his sword and he cuts himself free. He strikes the spider between the eyes, kills it, and falls back exhausted.

It is day when Bilbo wakes up and he sets off to look for the dwarves, feeling braver for having killed the spider. He decides to call his sword Sting. By chance he follows in the direction taken by his friends. Using his stealth and the protection of the ring, he is able to creep up on a gang of spiders who are discussing their captives, the dwarves, and anticipating the pleasure of eating them.

The dwarves are hanging in bundles from a high branch; one of the spiders nips the nose of the fattest bundle, Bombur, who kicks back at him. The spider is just about to kill Bombur when Bilbo hits it on the head with a stone and kills it. A second stone cuts the threads of a big web and sends another spider to its death. All the other spiders are now enraged and they rush in the direction from which the stones have come. Bilbo lures them away into the forest by singing an insulting song.

He returns to the place where the dwarves are held and kills the one remaining guard with his sword. He has freed all but five of the dwarves when the spiders return, and as they close in on him, Bilbo is horrified to see that Bombur is being dragged away. He rushes down from his branch to save Bombur and encourages all the other dwarves to leave the trees and fight on the ground. The plight of the dwarves seems hopeless as they become weaker and more tired. Eventually Bilbo decides to tell them the secret of his ring and to use his invisibility to draw the spiders off into the forest again, reappearing after a while to lead the dwarves in the last stages of the fight against the few remaining spiders.

When the spiders have given up, the dwarves find that they have wandered into an elf-ring where the spiders dare not enter. They rest here while Bilbo tells them the full story of the ring; their respect for him becomes so great that they look to Bilbo to find a way out of the forest. Suddenly Dwalin realises that Thorin is missing, having been captured in the night by the feasting wood-elves. Thorin has been taken to the cave on the edge of Mirkwood in which the elf-king lives and has been questioned about the reason for the dwarves being in Mirkwood. Thorin has refused to answer and now lies in the dungeon of the elf-king.

NOTES AND GLOSSARY:

**as they used a hundred years ago:** hobbits, of course, live a very long time

**the shape of a flying deer:** Tolkien may have derived this idea of a deer hunt in an enchanted forest from Book II of Edmund Spenser's (1552–99) *Faerie Queene* (1590) or from the medieval romance of *Sir Orfeo*

**span:** past tense of 'spin' (the usual form would be 'spun')

**hind:** female deer

**fawn:** a young deer

**the meaning of the hunt:** this is not a very clear reference but it is intended to indicate that the travellers are close to the land of the wood-elves, whose king lives in the east of Mirkwood, as we learn from the end of this chapter

**did not care tuppence:** did not care at all: 'tuppence' is short for 'two pence', a very small amount of money

**short commons:** inadequate food

**hark:** listen

**to be sure:** in truth

**bee-eautiful:** beautiful: spiders apparently speak slowly

**quoits . . . ninepins:** these are all games involving skill at aiming a missile at a stationary target. With the exception of 'shooting at the wand' these games are still played in England today

**attercop:** the Old English word for spider

**Tomnoddy:** an insulting name

**lazy . . . cob:** both 'cob' and 'lob' are words for spider

**still five dwarves:** Bilbo has rescued only seven dwarves, so the reader ought to be alert to the fact that one dwarf must be missing

**goggling:** staring at them in amazement

**it was from little Bilbo . . . answers:** this prepares us for the news that it is Thorin who is missing

**most of the trees were beeches:** after the dwarves had fired in vain at the white deer, they entered a part of the forest which consisted mostly of beeches: a further indication that they were close to the edge of Mirkwood

| | |
|---|---|
| **in ancient days . . . treasure:** | this prepares us for the dispute between the dwarves, the elves, and the men, over the treasures of the Lonely Mountain |
| **spell:** | enchantment |
| **thongs:** | strips of leather |

---

### Chapter 9: Barrels out of Bond

---

Bilbo and the dwarves try to find a path out of the forest and are set upon by wood elves: only Bilbo escapes and follows the elves and their prisoners into the cave of the Elvenking. The dwarves are questioned, as Thorin was, but they reveal nothing except their anger for the way in which they have been treated. Each is given food and drink and locked in a separate cell.

For many days Bilbo wanders through the passages of the cave and eventually discovers not only where each dwarf is kept, but also that Thorin is imprisoned within the dungeon. He talks to Thorin and takes secret messages to the other dwarves telling them not to reveal the reason for their journey through the wood. One day Bilbo finds an underground stream that flows out of the cave into the Forest River. Although it is blocked by a portcullis, the passage is often opened to allow in barrels of wine. Bilbo learns that this wine comes from the men of the Lake-town and that the empty barrels are allowed to float out of the castle to be collected downstream by the men.

One night when the chief guard is drunk, Bilbo steals his keys and releases the dwarves. After some reluctance they are persuaded to hide in the empty barrels. Bilbo does not even have time to think of his own means of escape before the elves come and push the barrels into the stream. Bilbo has no alternative but to cling on to the last barrel as it rolls into the water.

Eventually the current carries the barrels to the place where they are to be collected by the men. Bilbo uses his invisibility to steal food and drink from the men, and waits until the morning when the raft is once more pushed into the stream to continue its journey away from Mirkwood and on towards the Lake.

NOTES AND GLOSSARY:

| | |
|---|---|
| **had all he could do:** | was stretched to the limits of his ability |
| **Elvenking:** | king of the elves |
| **carven:** | the normal form would be 'carved' |
| **three times:** | the number three was held to be of special magical significance. See, for example, Shakespeare's *Macbeth*, where the three witches make three predictions about Macbeth's future |

**companies . . . ride out to hunt:** this is very similar to the presentation of the king of the underworld in the Medieval romance of *Sir Orfeo*

**had taken heart:**   had been encouraged

**portcullis:**   a kind of gate which opens vertically

**oaken trapdoor:**   trapdoor made of oak

**king's cellar:**   the cellars in a castle would be used to store wine. This feature, like the use of the term 'portcullis', emphasises that Tolkien is thinking of the Elven-king's stronghold as a medieval castle

**throve:**   prospered. The usual form of the past tense for the verb 'thrive' would be 'thrived'

**very good . . . send up poor stuff:** the chief of the guards is not very concerned about the quality of wine to be drunk at the king's tables. His real desire is to find an excuse to sample the wine for himself

**all in a flutter:**   very agitated

**flagons:**   large jugs

**heady:**   potent, intoxicating

**Dorwinion:**   this place is not mentioned elsewhere in Tolkien's works

**drat:**   curse

**king's fold:**   the king's people

**how the dwarves would take it:** how the dwarves would react to it

**the old slowcoach:**   the slow old fellow

**small wonder:**   it is no surprise

**turnkey:**   jailer: he who turns the key

**toss-pot:**   drunkard

**heave-ho:**   an expression which frequently occurs in work-songs, such as sea-shanties, which accompany strenuous effort

**down into the water:** it was made very clear in Chapter 5 that Bilbo was terrified of the water. Thus his bravery here is the greater

**you cannot count:**   you cannot regard as significant

**eddying:**   moving with a swirling, circular motion

**shingly shore:**   a shore composed of shingle (small pebbles) rather than sand

## Chapter 10: A Warm Welcome

As the day grows lighter Bilbo catches his first sight of the Lonely Mountain, and learns from listening to the raftmen that he has arrived there by the only workable route. When the barrels arrive at the Lake-town the raft is moored while the men and the elves go into the town. Bilbo uses this opportunity to cut loose the barrels containing the dwarves and to bring them, one by one, to the shore.

Bilbo, Thorin, Fili, and Kili set off for Lake-town where they surprise the guards and demand to see the Master of the town, who is at a feast with the raftman and the elves. Although Thorin claims to be grandson of Thror, King under the Mountain, the elves recognise him as an escaped prisoner. The people of the Lake-town are so excited at Thorin's arrival, however, that they sing of the return of the King under the Mountain, and the Master is forced to go along with Thorin's story. The other dwarves are brought to the town and are well fed. The elves, meanwhile, return to the palace of the Elvenking, who suspects that the real purpose of Bilbo and the dwarves is to find treasure in the Lonely Mountain and not (as the people of the Lake-town think) to kill the dragon Smaug.

Bilbo and the dwarves stay for two weeks with the people of the Lake-town until, equipped with boats and provisions, they set out for the Mountain.

NOTES AND GLOSSARY:

**dark head in a torn cloud:** a poetic description of the way in which the summit of the mountain sticks through the cloud, as if it is tearing the cloud

**loomed:** appeared threateningly

**to attribute to the dragon ... Mountain:** superstitious people in England believe that to name Satan directly is dangerous. If the need arises they will only refer to him obliquely. Tolkien is basing the behaviour of the Lakemen on this same principle

**the skirts:** the edges

**other business ... tale:** a further allusion to the fact that there might be other legends in which Gandalf plays a part

**the Wain:** a group of seven bright stars, more usually known as the Great Bear. Tolkien's use of this name follows the practice of early English writers including Chaucer, the great poet and astronomer, who lived in the fourteenth century

**Thror and Thrain:** these names of former dwarf kings were first mentioned in the opening chapter of the book

**famished:** ravaged by hunger

**floundering:** thrashing around without any sense of purpose

**thank our stars:** thank our luck. Some superstitious people believe that certain movements of the planets and the stars can have an effect upon the lives of men

**river-tolls:** money paid in order to have access to the waterway
**gammers:** old men, grandfathers
**the unpacking of the dwarves:** the releasing of the dwarves from the casks by Bilbo
**sons of my father's daughters:** the relationship between a man and the sons of his sisters is a particularly close bond in the heroic code on which *The Hobbit* was based; see p.13
**vagabond:** rough, unemployed, and homeless person
**give any good account:** give any explanation
**waylaid:** captured
**carven stone:** carved stone
**upholden:** held up high (in triumph)
**harp:** this is the instrument most frequently used in early English literature to represent the harmony and pleasure to be derived from music
**songs of yore:** songs of long ago
**where he came in:** how he fitted into Thorin's company and to the predictions of the songs
**thag you very buch.:** the effect of a cold in the head is to make the pronunciation of certain sounds difficult. It is this difficulty which Tolkien is trying to represent here
**fortnight:** two weeks
**laden:** loaded down
**circuitous:** describing many twists and turns

## Chapter 11: On the Doorstep

After three days on the river the travellers disembark and are met by the men and the ponies bringing up their provisions from Lake-town. The men depart immediately, afraid of the dragon, and the travellers are left unprotected once again. The aim of the company is to discover the hidden door in the west of the mountain, but Thorin first sends a scouting party (Balin, Fili, Kili, and Bilbo) to investigate the Front Gate to the south. They see there the ruins of the town of Dale, now quite desolate, with the only movement in the landscape being the smoke rising from the mountain and the ominous crows in the sky.

For many days the dwarves search for the secret door, making their camp on the western side of the mountain. At last, after many unsuccessful sorties, Bilbo comes across a flight of rough steps leading to a narrow ledge on the top of a cliff. Bilbo, Fili, and Kili explore this ledge and discover a sheltered bay at the end of which is a sheer wall of rock. This, they decide, must be the door.

There is no way, however, that either Bilbo or the dwarves can open the door, even when most of the party have been brought up from the camp. As the days go by the dwarves expect Bilbo to discover a solution, which only serves to increase his misery. Suddenly, after a whole day of thinking, Bilbo notices a thrush eating a snail by the light of the setting sun and he is reminded, by the cracking of the shell, of Elrond and the moon letters which he found on the map. Bilbo alerts the others and they all watch as the last ray of the sun strikes the wall. As the thrush trills, a crack in the wall reveals a hole into which Thorin places his key. The dwarves push hard on the rock and the doorway opens up.

NOTES AND GLOSSARY:

**the waning of the year:** the end of the year, when plants have ceased to grow

**spur:** a ridge of land projecting away from the mountain

**Ravenhill:** the origin of this name is made clear in Chapter 15

**exposed:** open to attack

**the day the Dragon came:** the events of this day have been told already in Chapter 1

**the waste:** the barren land of the Desolation

**foul reek:** foul smell

**broken spells of opening:** incantations designed to open the door. (The most famous 'spell of opening' is 'open sesame' from *The Arabian Night*)

**you would be thirteen again:** as they would have been if they had not persuaded Bilbo to join them

**spoke low:** spoke quietly

**much brighter:** much happier

**next year after that:** until the sixteenth century English calendars made March the first month of the year, so that the year began with the springtime

**hailed:** shouted to

## Chapter 12: Inside Information

Thorin decides that Bilbo should go first through the doorway, and only Balin is prepared to go with him. Once inside they discover a well-made passage leading into the heart of the mountain. After a while Bilbo is left to continue on his own, wearing the ring, while Balin stays as a look-out. As he moves onwards Bilbo starts to feel warmer and a red glow ahead of him becomes increasingly brighter. Finally he hears the snoring of an animal and realises that he is about to enter the cave of the sleeping Smaug. Summoning all his courage, Bilbo enters the treasure-filled cave and, after gazing in wonder for a time, he takes a cup, intending to take it back with him to show the dwarves. Smaug stirs in his sleep but does not wake, and Bilbo is able to escape to the safety of Balin and the other dwarves.

Bilbo is still receiving the congratulations of the dwarves when a great rumbling from the mountain reveals that the dragon has woken from his sleep and has realised that the cup is missing. In his rage Smaug rushes out of the Front Gate and into the air, searching for the thief who has stolen his cup.

Bilbo advises the dwarves to hide in the tunnel after they have hauled up Bombur and Bofur from the camp in the valley below. The dwarves hide in the tunnel as the fires of Smaug rage outside throughout the night. Finally Smaug returns exhausted to his lair. Flight is now impossible for the travellers because they have lost their ponies, and once again the dwarves blame Bilbo for their misfortunes. He volunteers to use his magic ring to pay another visit to Smaug's cave to try to discover whether the dragon has any weak spot which the dwarves can exploit to destroy him.

When Bilbo returns to Smaug he finds the dragon feigning sleep and becomes involved in a conversation with him. Although Bilbo is invisible the dragon can smell him, and Bilbo has to use all his resources to stop himself falling under the spell of the dragon's enchanting words. Bilbo is able to flatter the dragon into revealing an unprotected area of his body in his left breast before he seizes the opportunity to escape back up the tunnel. Smaug is too big to follow Bilbo through this narrow space.

When he reaches the safety of his friends once more Bilbo is annoyed with himself for having revealed so much to the dragon and in his anger he throws a stone at a thrush. Bilbo again persuades the dwarves to take shelter in the tunnel, for he is convinced that Smaug will now do everything in his power to find and destroy them. In the tunnel the dwarves talk of the treasure of Smaug's cavern and in particular of the Arkenstone, a great jewel from the heart of the mountain. In the nick of time Bilbo urges the dwarves to close the door of the tunnel for they can hear rocks falling outside as Smaug heaps boulders on the side of the mountain. The dragon has worked out that Bilbo must have had the help of the men from the Lake-town in order to have reached the mountain, and he prepares to exact revenge from them.

NOTES AND GLOSSARY:

**what he was driving at:** what he meant

**third time pays for all:** a variation on the gambling expression 'third time lucky'

**more than hobbit's care:** we are already aware of the ability which hobbits have to move silently

**put your foot in it:** made a rash and impetuous decision

**thrumming:** regular rhythmic noise

**wrought and unwrought:** either made into objects or still in its unworked state

**coats of mail:** protective coats made of interlinked rings of metal

**helms:** helmets

**Bilbo's breath was taken away:** Bilbo was astonished

**staggerment:** a word of Tolkien's own invention meaning 'astonishment'

**dire:** terrible

**not yet:** Tolkien whets our appetite for the time when Smaug will wake

**to be reckoned with:** not to be forgotten or dismissed

**rumour:** distant noise

**Mr Baggins:** the fact that Thorin uses this form of address indicates the extent of his politeness

**Every worm has his weak spot:** Tolkien invents this proverb. 'Worm' in this context means 'dragon'

**dragon-lore:** knowledge about dragons

**Smaug the Tremendous:** Bilbo deliberately chooses exaggerated terms of praise in order to flatter Smaug

**clue-finder:** Bilbo found the clue that led to the opening of the secret door

**the web-cutter:** an allusion to Bilbo's fight against the spiders

**the stinging fly:** Bilbo's knife is called Sting

**chosen for the lucky number:** without Bilbo there would have been a company of thirteen (see p.17)

**he that buries . . . from the water:** an allusion to the way in which Bilbo rescued the dwarves from the capture of the elves

**from the end of a bag:** Bilbo's home is Bag-End

**friend of bears:** the friend of Beorn

**or I'm a lizard:** it is commonplace to assert one's faith in a particular opinion by saying 'It is true, or I'm a monkey's uncle'. Tolkien adapts the expression to something more appropriate to the dragon

**Esgaroth:** the Lake-town

**Girion Lord of Dale:** Smaug speaks of the line of kings of men who used to live in Dale

**it became a favourite saying:** we are not allowed to wonder whether Bilbo will escape safely. This remark makes it clear that he will live through this adventure

**tame to the hands:** unafraid of; trained by

**the Arkenstone:** in Old English 'eorcanstan' meant 'precious stone'

**marrow:** the very centre of the bones

**jumble of smithereens:** confusion of tiny fragments

## Chapter 13: Not at Home

Trapped inside the tunnel the dwarves are thoroughly miserable, but Bilbo offers to lead them out by taking them right through the dragon's cavern. All is darkness at the end of the tunnel and Bilbo falls over. He realises that Smaug must have left his lair and he persuades the dwarves to light torches. Because the dwarves will not enter the cave until he has explored it, Bilbo is alone when he discovers the Arkenstone and he puts it secretly into his pocket. The dwarves, when they finally pluck up courage to enter the cave, are astonished at the beauty and the value of the treasure. They persuade Bilbo to put on a coat of *mithril*, and they dress themselves in splendid armour. It is all Bilbo can do to convince the dwarves that they must leave the cavern and find a way out of the mountain. Fortunately Thorin remembers the place well from his youth and they follow him to the Front Gate. Although they are all tired and hungry, they march on through the Desolation until they reach the relative security of the look-out tower at Ravenhill. There they rest, wondering all the while what Smaug might be doing.

NOTES AND GLOSSARY:

**his wits:**            his powers of reason

**grumpy:**             irritated

**who had small interest in music:** the dragon wants only to own objects, not to make use of them in any way

**mithril:**             this substance is described more fully in *The Lord of the Rings* (Book II, Chapter 4)

**looking-glass:**     mirror

**mouldered:**         decayed

**a road running towards Ravenhill:** this location was mentioned at the beginning of Chapter 11

**cram:**              an apt name for a food which is intended to fill the stomach rather than to please the taste

## Chapter 14: Fire and Water

The men of the Lake-town had at first been excited to see light coming from the Lonely Mountain, for some had felt that it signalled the victory of Thorin. Soon, however, they realised that it heralded the approach of the dragon. Smaug was unable to cross the bridge to the town because the Master had ordered it to be cut, so he could only fly over the rooftops setting fire to buildings and terrifying the inhabitants. Some of these, including the Master himself, tried to save themselves by taking to the water, but this was precisely what Smaug hoped for: small boats were an easy prey. One man on the island encouraged the others to stay and fight. This man, Bard, was told by an old thrush that the dragon was vulnerable under its left breast and, as the dragon circled over the town, Bard shot his black arrow, which had never failed him, and he killed Smaug. The town, however, was completely ruined by the fall of the dragon's body.

The people of the town were unhappy at the loss of their property and at the cowardice of the Master. They wished to choose Bard as their king and were not dissuaded by the Master, who blamed Thorin for rousing the anger of the dragon. Finally Bard promised to continue to serve the Master and he set about organising the building of shelters for the townspeople. He was helped in this work by the Elvenking who, hearing of the death of Smaug, was marching north to look for treasure in the mountain. A new town was built by the shore, where the Master remained with the women and children while Bard led the rest of the men to join the elves on their march to the mountain.

NOTES AND GLOSSARY:

| | |
|---|---|
| **dart:** | spear |
| **Bard:** | 'bard' is a word for poet in old English |
| **gilded:** | decorated with gold |
| **black arrow:** | in 1893 Robert Louis Stevenson (1850–94), the Scottish novelist, wrote a book for boys called *The Black Arrow* |
| **gledes:** | embers, fire |
| **It is an ill wind . . . any good:** | a proverbial expression meaning that even the worst misfortune will hold profit for somebody |

---

## Chapter 15: The Gathering of the Clouds

---

Bilbo and the dwarves spend the night on the rock tower without seeing any sign of the dragon. In the morning a great flock of birds from the south arrives at Ravenhill, including the old thrush from the mountain. The dwarves are unable to understand the message brought by the thrush, even though Balin claims that he was once friendly with an old raven who used to live on the very rock tower on which they are at present encamped. The thrush flies off to return with an old raven who proves to be the son of the bird which Balin knew. From Roäc, the raven, they learn that Smaug is dead, but their joy is tempered by the news that elves and men are on their way to lay claim to the dragon's treasure. Roäc warns them that the Master is not to be trusted, although Bard is an honest man. Thorin thanks the raven and asks him to bring further news, and also to send word to the dwarves in the north that Thorin needs their aid.

The dwarves work hard to fortify the mountain against attack, blocking the Front Gate and damming the stream to form a pool. They are fortunate in finding three of their ponies unharmed, thus recovering some of their provisions.

One night the mountain is lit by the torches of approaching elves and men. Thorin asks them what they want but there is no reply. The invaders make camp and sing songs so beautiful that Bilbo (and even some of the dwarves) begin to wish that they could be at peace with their enemies. The dwarves sing a song themselves which celebrates the return of the King under the Mountain. This pleases Thorin who thinks of the help which is on its way from his cousin Dain in the north.

On the following morning Thorin and Bard start their negotiations. Bilbo can see the justice in Bard's claim to a share of the treasure for four reasons: because Bard has slain Smaug; because the dragon's hoard includes goods stolen from Bard's people; because Smaug has destroyed Esgaroth; and because the men of the town helped the dwarves when they were in need. Thorin, however, has become affected by a lust for wealth and he refuses to accept that the men have any claim to the treasure. He promises to pay for the assistance the dwarves were given, but not until the men and the elves have withdrawn from the mountain and not while the men are in league with the Elvenking.

Later a messenger from Bard asks Thorin to yield one-twelfth of the treasure to Bard as the dragon-slayer, but he is answered only by an arrow from Thorin. The messenger declares the mountain besieged, and the dwarves are left alone.

NOTES AND GLOSSARY:

**autumn wanderings:** some European birds migrate in early autumn to spend the winter in warmer climates. Thorin knows that it is too late in the year for this to be the cause of these birds' flight; and he realises that, in any event, these are not birds which ever migrate

**Dain:** another name taken from the Icelandic *Prose Edda*

**a parley:** a formal debate or negotiation between enemies: from the French *parlez* (speak)

**though doubtless undesigned:** Bard shows generosity in adding this final phrase, absolving the dwarves from direct responsibility for the destruction of Esgaroth

**with small kindness:** with little gratitude or affection

**succoured:** aided

---

### Chapter 16: A Thief in the Night

---

Under siege, the dwarves pass their time by searching through the treasure, looking particularly for the Arkenstone. Thorin threatens to kill anybody who conceals it from him. News arrives that Dain is on his way, but even this does not cheer the dwarves greatly, for they cannot see how they can raise the siege and still find food to last them through the winter.

Bilbo, at first worried about having the Arkenstone in his possession, at last devises a plan to make use of it. He offers to take Bombur's turn at the watch, and using the invisibility of the ring, he slips into the enemy camp and surrenders himself. He tells Bard that Dain is on his way and gives him the Arkenstone to use in bargaining with Thorin. As he leaves the camp to go back to the mountain he meets Gandalf, who congratulates him on his enterprise. Safe inside the mountain once again, Bilbo falls soundly asleep.

NOTES AND GLOSSARY:

**tattered oddments:** torn pieces of old cloth

**a dwarf with a stiff neck:** a stubborn dwarf

**recapture the beautiful dreams:** the dreams that he had after falling in the stream in Mirkwood (Chapter 8)

**the dwarves' hobbit:** the phrase suggests that the dwarves own Bilbo. His reply asserts his own independence and dignity

**share in the profits:** Bilbo is not to receive a fourteenth share of the treasure, but only a share of the profits of the total expedition

**not without a shudder:** the reluctance that Bilbo feels to part with the jewel is the basis of the attachment which Tolkien is to depict as characteristic of those who wear the ring in *The Lord of the Rings*

## Chapter 17: The Clouds Burst

In the morning another messenger from the camp arrives to ask if Thorin believes the new event to be the imminent arrival of Dain and agrees to parley. When Bard arrives, however, he asks if Thorin is prepared to surrender gold in return for the Arkenstone, which he has with him in a casket. Thorin is furious that the jewel has fallen into the hands of his enemies, and further enraged when Bilbo admits to having given it to Bard. Bilbo claims that he took the stone as his share of the hoard, and he is supported by Gandalf, who now reveals himself among Bard's party.

Thorin curses Bilbo and casts him out from the mountain. He agrees that on the following day he will surrender a fourteenth share of the treasure to Bard in return for the Arkenstone, but already he is plotting a way to keep both the stone and the treasure, and he sends a message to Dain to warn him to approach with caution.

On the following morning Dain and his dwarves arrive in the valley near Bard's camp. Bard refuses to allow Dain to join his cousin until the gold has been paid, but now Thorin sends out only arrows at Bard's messengers. As Bard and the Elvenking debate whether they should wage battle on the dwarves, the dwarves themselves mount an attack.

However, this battle is short-lived as Gandalf sees the approach of a new common enemy—the goblins: hated by elves, men, and dwarves. Having heard of the fall of Smaug, the goblins hope for the opportunity to take control of the land. The Elvenking, Bard, and Dain decide together to lure the goblins into the valley and then to attack from the spurs above them.

The plan is successful initially as the goblins are charged first by the elves and then by the dwarves; but some of the goblins climb the mountain from the other side and the battle seems to be going to them. At this point Thorin leads a charge from out of the mountain which attacks even the fearsome bodyguard of the goblin's king, Bolg.

But Thorin's army is too small and Bilbo is convinced that the goblins will triumph in the end, when suddenly he sees a host of eagles flocking to the mountain. As he cries out in delight he is knocked unconscious by a falling rock, and knows no more.

NOTES AND GLOSSARY:

**got wind of:** heard rumours of
**heirloom:** an object transferred by inheritance from one generation of a family to another
**take it that:** understand it to mean that
**hauberk:** armour worn to protect the neck
**mattocks:** axe-like weapons with a large blade
**were shod with iron:** had iron shoes
**long will I tarry:** I will wait for a long time
**how it fell out:** how it came about
**nimblest:** most athletic
**scimitars:** large swords with curved blades
**the more Tookish part:** the part that loved adventure (see Chapter 1 for an explanation of Bilbo's ancestry)
**misery me:** alas
**well out of it:** glad to be finished with the whole business

## Chapter 18: The Return Journey

Bilbo regains consciousness to find the battle over. He is taken by a man to a tent in which Gandalf tends the dying Thorin, whose last words are of friendship with Bilbo. Gandalf tells him how the battle ended: the eagles drove the goblins from the mountain with the support of Beorn, who not only carried the wounded Thorin to safety, but also drove off the goblins altogether. Fili and Kili died with Thorin in battle.

The Arkenstone is placed on Thorin's breast as he is laid to rest deep in the mountain, and the Elvenking returns to Thorin's body the sword which he took from him earlier. Dain becomes King under the Mountain and supervises the distribution of the treasure. Bilbo refuses to take more than two small chests (one of silver and one of gold) and he bids farewell to the dwarves. Gandalf and Bilbo ride with the Elvenking as far as Mirkwood and then make their way west, staying with Beorn until the spring comes again.

NOTES AND GLOSSARY:
**rent armour:** torn armour
**take back my words:** deny that I meant what I said
**their mother's eldest brother:** on the bonds of this relationship, see the note on p.37
**Yule-tide:** Christmas-time

---

## Chapter 19: The Last Stage

---

Gandalf and Bilbo arrive at Rivendell where the elves are anxious for news of their adventure. Gandalf reveals that he has been to a council of wizards and that they have driven the Necromancer from Mirkwood, although he has not been entirely destroyed.

After their rest at Rivendell the two journey back to Hobbiton and discover the gold of the trolls on the way. When they arrive at Bag-End it is being stripped of its furniture by Bilbo's cousins, who have assumed that he is dead. Bilbo stops them, although he never recovers all his property. Throughout the rest of his life Bilbo is regarded with suspicion by his neighbours, but he lives happily writing poetry, drafting his memoirs, and visiting the elves. One evening he is visited by Gandalf and Balin, and Bilbo learns that Dale has been rebuilt with Bard as its King; that Esgaroth is now prosperous and has a new, wiser Master; and that the desolation surrounding the mountain is no longer barren. Everywhere is at peace.

NOTES AND GLOSSARY:
**the gloaming:** the evening, twilight
**whither so laden:** where are you going with such a load
**our back is to the legends:** the legends are all over
**share and share alike:** let each of us have equal shares
**from next to nothing to old songs:** very little money
**his nephews . . . Took side:** this branch of Bilbo's family is to play a prominent role in *The Lord of the Rings*

# Part 3

# Commentary

## *The Hobbit* and *The Lord of the Rings*

*The Hobbit* was published on 21 September 1937 but then it had been in existence for some six or seven years. It began as a story read by Tolkien to his own children, although some of Tolkien's friends also heard parts of it, and C.S. Lewis had read most of the book in typescript form in 1932.* It appears that the part of the work which caused its writer most difficulty was the conclusion, and we shall examine below the argument that Tolkien developed the book as he was writing the final version, taking it away from its origins as a children's story towards a work more adult in tone and theme.

The book was accepted for publication by Allen & Unwin on the strength of the recommendation of Rayner Unwin, the ten-year-old son of the chairman.† It was such a success that Tolkien was pressed by his publisher to produce more books about hobbits, but it was not until 1954 that he finally published the first volume of his trilogy *The Lord of the Rings*—which was to extend his treatment of the hobbits much further than his publishers had dreamed of.

It would be most inaccurate to describe *The Lord of the Rings* as a sequel to *The Hobbit*. It is true that the trilogy takes up its narrative some time after the return of Bilbo Baggins from his quest, but it does not become a description of similar adventures to the quest for Thorin's treasure. *The Lord of the Rings* is not presented as a story for children and has, in consequence, received a much larger share of critical attention than *The Hobbit*. In terms of their broad structure the two works have some similarity: each begins with a party; each involves a journey there and back again; each journey lasts a full year.‡ But the differences between the works are more marked than their similarities, and may be typified by comparing the reasons which lead the two hobbit-heroes to embark on their quests. Bilbo goes as a matter of pride, and on a sudden

---

*Full details of the circumstances of composition of *The Hobbit* can be found in H. CARPENTER: *J.R.R. Tolkien*, Allen & Unwin, London, 1977, pp.177–82.
†Rayner Unwin's review is reproduced in *The Hobbit*, introduced by R.S. Fowler, Allen & Unwin, London, 1972, p.301.
‡There is detailed comparison of *The Hobbit* and *The Lord of the Rings* in Randel Helms, *Tolkien's World*, Thames & Hudson, London, 1974, Chapter 2; and in Paul Kocher, *Master of Middle-earth*, Thames & Hudson, London, 1972, pp.26–33.

impulse. His reasons are frivolous and we cannot take his quest seriously for the first few chapters. When Frodo Baggins leaves at the start of *The Lord of the Rings*, however, 'he goes with the pain of a sad but noble decision, bearing with him the fate of an entire world.'* There is never a chance that we will think Frodo's quest lightly undertaken or ridiculous in execution.

Randel Helms has effectively summarised the differences between *The Hobbit* and *The Lord of the Rings* and it remains only to point out that although the works might appear to share common features (Gollum and the Ring appear in both, for example), these features have been so altered in the later work that a reading of *The Lord of the Rings* might do more to confuse than to help the student whose primary interest is in *The Hobbit*. For the serious student of Tolkien's fiction, however, a reading of *The Lord of the Rings* is indispensable.

# The hobbit

The novel is called *The Hobbit* and Tolkien lays emphasis on the fact that his hero is not only Bilbo Baggins, but also a member of a particular species. The elves, dwarves, and goblins in the book are not creatures of Tolkien's own invention; and many of the characteristics which they possess are to be found associated with them elsewhere in literature and in mythology. Hobbits, however, are Tolkien's own creatures, and we need to examine carefully what kind of being he has created for his hero.

Tolkien is well aware that hobbits will be unknown to his readers and so he explains their physical characteristics fully in the opening chapter of the book. This description leaves unanswered the reader's curiosity about what a hobbit might do, how he might feel, and how he might behave. Tolkien's description of hobbits makes them appear sufficiently like men for us to suspect that they might act as we do, inspired by the same motives and a similar notion of what is good and what is bad. Yet it is clear from the beginning of the book that hobbits are not people, and thus our interest is maintained in finding out how the species will behave.

Hobbits are new to us and we are interested to see what a hobbit can do. Within the book, however, hobbits are made to seem new to many of the other creatures in Tolkien's world. Neither the trolls nor Smaug have ever encountered a hobbit before, although they know well enough what a dwarf might be. It is not merely Bilbo Baggins who is unadventurous and comfortable in his quiet life: the hobbit race as a whole shares these characteristics.

Bilbo is very much an isolated figure, one whose true quality is untested at the start of the book, and cannot be taken for granted. He is

*\* Tolkien's World*, ibid, p.32.

the only hobbit of any significance in the book (whereas *The Lord of the Rings* includes a number of hobbits in its central set of characters): he is *the* hobbit in a company of dwarves. Dwarves as a race are presented as frequent and accustomed adventurers: there are songs sung in the Lake-town of the return of the King under the Mountain, but no mention is made of how a hobbit might be involved. Bilbo is even described by the elves in Chapter 16 as 'the dwarves' hobbit', a servant of the dwarves. His task in the course of the book is to demonstrate not only what he can do as an individual but also to show the capacities of hobbits in general. Gandalf's prophecy in Chapter 1—'There is a lot more in him than you can guess, and a deal more than he has any idea of himself'—applies equally well to our expectations about hobbits as a race as it does to Bilbo himself: we as readers cannot guess what hobbits might do, any more than the dwarves or elves within the book can guess.

A number of different explanations have been suggested for Tolkien's choice of the name 'hobbit' for his invented race. Edmund Wilson unkindly suggested that the name was a combination of 'hob' (a rustic) and 'rabbit', an explanation not very far from Tolkien's own explanation of the derivation of the name, which came from an Old English word 'holbytla' meaning 'hole dweller'.* A more likely explanation is cited in Humphrey Carpenter's biography of Tolkien in which he records that Tolkien once told an interviewer that the name hobbit: 'might have been associated with Sinclair Lewis's Babbitt . . . Babbitt has the same bourgeois smugness that hobbits do. His world is the same limited place.'† It is certainly true that Sinclair Lewis (1885–1951), an American novelist, produced in *Babbitt* (1922) a work that shares with *The Hobbit* the notion of having a central figure who seems to be anything but heroic.

Tolkien freely admitted that he himself had many of the characteristics of a hobbit: he smoked a pipe, liked a life of comfort, disliked travel, and wore ornamented waistcoats.‡ It may well be more than a coincidence that he gives to Bilbo's more adventurous ancestors, the Tooks, a name not unlike his own.

*The Hobbit* gives us a clear picture of the characteristics of Bilbo Baggins. He is presented in the opening chapter as an amusing, rather self-indulgent creature, too fond of his comfortable existence; wary of strangers; too concerned about the neatness of his home; with an appetite for food which borders on gluttony. But the journey with the dwarves brings out other qualities in him. His ability to move quietly

---

*E. WILSON: 'Oo, Those Awful Orcs!', *Nation*, CLXXXII, No.15, April 14 1956, pp.312–14.
†H. CARPENTER, *J.R.R. Tolkien*, Allen & Unwin, London, 1977, p.165.
‡*J.R.R. Tolkien*, ibid, p.176.

makes him an appropriate 'burglar' and is a quality which serves to his advantage throughout the book. He feels pity for Gollum, and appreciates that Bard may indeed have a claim on Smaug's treasure. He shows considerable bravery both when alone and when required to save his companions from danger. Above all, like Tolkien himself, Bilbo delights in poetry.

From the opening chapter of the book Tolkien emphasises that Bilbo appreciates the beauty of art: 'As they sang the hobbit felt the love of beautiful things made by hands and by cunning and by magic.' Tolkien felt that art in general and poetry in particular was a mark of the civilisation of man. He objected to those critics of poetry who failed to appreciate the beauty of the work because they were so concerned with what a poem might tell them of history or geography.* In *Beowulf*, the early English epic which Tolkien loved, the monster Grendel is driven into a frenzy because he hears men singing. He has no gift of song, no art, and is therefore driven to destroy theirs. Poetry symbolised for Tolkien a fragile beauty which could easily be destroyed by those who failed to appreciate its worth (and this included the thoughtless, insensitive critic).

In *The Hobbit* poetry and song have a key role to play. The dwarves have music and their songs play upon Bilbo's imagination. In contrast, the goblins sing terrifying songs of destruction and ruin. Music is therefore shown to be a force for good, for harmony, which can be perverted to evil ends. Like wealth or power, music can be used or abused, depending on who is playing it. In the Lake-town there are men who are responsive to songs and others who are not. Despite the popular legends of the King under the Mountain, 'some of the younger people in the town openly doubted the existence of any dragon in the mountain' (Chapter 10). The book proves that these young people are wrong to doubt the truth of the myth, and therefore implies that those who fail to believe in legends, those who are unmoved by poetry, are misguided and are failing to realise their full potential. At the end of *The Hobbit* Bilbo himself takes to writing poetry but, although it makes him very happy, he is regarded by his fellow hobbits as quite mad.† It seems that in this respect Bilbo is exceptional: not all hobbits appreciate the beauties of poetry.

The episode which demonstrates most clearly that an appreciation of beauty is the mark of civilisation, is the winning of Smaug's treasure near the end of the book. Smaug is identified as uncivilised because he has no use for the objects in his possession. They represent only wealth,

*The thesis that Tolkien's fiction is concerned with the relationship between art and its attackers is advanced in JANE CHANCE NITZSCHE: *Tolkien's Art*, Macmillan, London, 1979.
†P. KOCHER: *Master of Middle-Earth*, Thames & Hudson, London, 1972, p.26.

not beauty. The harps which Fili and Kili discover in the hoard have never been touched by Smaug, because the dragon has no interest in music. In contrast, those who lay claim to the treasure all share a love of music which makes the reader feel that they should not be fighting against one another. As the elves sit in their camp outside the Lonely Mountain:

> There was the sound . . . of elven harps and of sweet music; and as it echoed up towards them it seemed that the chill of the air was warmed, and they caught faintly the fragrance of woodland flowers blossoming in spring.
> Then Bilbo longed to escape from the dark fortress and . . . join in the mirth and feasting by the fires. Some of the younger dwarves . . . muttered that they wished things had fallen out otherwise and that they might welcome such folk as friends, but Thorin scowled.
> (Chapter 15)

Bilbo and the younger dwarves know that they have a great deal in common with the elves, including an appreciation of the beauty of song. The fact that Thorin is insensitive to this is one indication of his corruption at this stage of the book. He is becoming like Smaug, an enemy to civilisation.

## There and Back Again

The full title Tolkien gave to his first novel was *The Hobbit, or There and Back Again* and the alternative title indicates something of the structure of the book. It is a quest story, an example of a kind of narrative in which the central character is obliged to go on a journey in search of a particular object or person. The book, however, does not divide neatly into two sections—one for the outward journey and a second for the return home—nor does the quest develop as simply as it might have done. It would have been possible to have confined the story to the winning of Smaug's treasure and Bilbo's subsequent return. In fact there is some evidence that Tolkien intended to write such a story, with Bilbo killing Smaug himself.* *The Hobbit* is not so simple and Tolkien seems to have changed his mind about the book during the time it took him to prepare the published version.

The opening chapters of the book give a rather misleading impression of what the dominant tone of the work is finally to be. It seems that the quest is to be quite uncomplicated, even though it is to be dangerous. Bilbo and the dwarves are to re-possess the treasures of the Lonely Mountain. There is no discussion of what they will do when they have

*H. CARPENTER: *J.R.R. Tolkien*, Allen & Unwin, London, 1977, p.179.

it, nor how they expect to return home safely with it. Moreover, the quest is a totally material venture: there is no question, in the opening chapter, of Thorin's ambition to be King under the Mountain in place of Smaug, nor of the need for Smaug to be killed.

It is in these early chapters that the book is most obviously a tale for children, and this is clear in the narrator's asides as well as in the attempts at humour. We are not allowed to forget that there is a narrator in these first chapters, because he keeps involving himself in the story by talking directly to the reader: 'The mother of our particular hobbit —what is a hobbit? I suppose hobbits need some description nowadays. . . . Now you know enough to go on with' (Chapter 1). The way in which the narrator addresses the reader at this point makes it obvious that the reader is thought of as being a child, with a child's innocence and curiosity. The humour in the opening chapters is similarly addressed to childish taste: the arrival of the dwarves at Bilbo's door owes a good deal in its telling to nursery tales, and even Thorin speaks with ridiculous and exaggerated gravity: 'We are met together in the house of our friend and fellow conspirator, this most excellent and audacious hobbit—may the hairs on his toes never fall out!' (Chapter 1) This is very different from the way in which the leader of the dwarves might be expected to speak in *The Lord of the Rings*; but more significantly, it is different from the way in which Thorin speaks later in this book. In the first chapters of *The Hobbit* Tolkien presents what appears to be the opening to a children's story, with delightful and amusing creatures setting off into the unknown on an adventure which will be fun and will bring them a definite prize: Smaug's treasure.

The reader and the dwarves are in a very similar situation at the beginning of the book. Like the reader, the dwarves are treated as childlike and naive, failing to play adequately for the rigours of the adventure, not thinking ahead but treating it merely as fun. The reader, like the dwarves, is led to believe that Bilbo is an inappropriate member of the company and that he is a somewhat ridiculous fellow. His chief characteristic seems to be a greed for food: 'he was just sitting down to a nice little second breakfast' (Chapter 2) which is hardly a trait associated with the hero of an adventure. Yet Bilbo's concern for food and shelter is to be an essential part of the development of the book. Even heroes need to eat and, as Bilbo becomes increasingly prepared to go for long periods without food, so the dwarves appreciate the need to pay attention to such practical matters. Bilbo may be greedy in his eating (and even here he is presented as courteous, if rather unwilling, in his treatment of his guests: he knows that their needs take precedence over his), but he is generous in every other respect, and is certainly not possessive about material objects.

It would not be inaccurate to describe *The Hobbit* as a story of greed and possession. Bilbo's love of food is set against the lust that other creatures have for possessions, and the way in which they can become corrupted by this lust. Bilbo is employed by the dwarves quite specifically as a burglar, and we may have doubts from the beginning of the book about this employment: burglars, after all, are outside the law and act against any system of morals. We may wonder how the central figure of a novel can pursue such an occupation and still be positively presented. Initially our doubts are easily dispelled, because Bilbo's thefts are always from wicked creatures: we cannot feel uneasy at his stealing from the trolls, for example. The situation is much more complex in the case of the treasure of the Lonely Mountain, however, for it is by no means clear who has a right to share the spoils.

Our attitude to the quest changes in the course of the book: we no longer feel that the gaining of the treasure is of paramount importance. We are more interested in the use to which the treasure may be put, and in whether the characters in the book can keep their desire for property in check. As the spokesman for the elves says to Thorin: 'I declare the Mountain beseiged. You shall not depart from it, until you call on your side for a truce and a parley. We will bear no weapons against you, but we leave you to your gold. You may eat that, if you will!' (Chapter 15). The elves do not need to bear arms against the dwarves, Thorin's own greed for gold is enough to destroy him.

# Eating gold

*The Hobbit* contains a wide range of creatures, introduced by Tolkien as they are encountered by Bilbo and the dwarves on their way to the Lonely Mountain. In the first part of the book there is a regular alternation of foes and friends (the trolls are bad, Elrond's elves are good, the goblins wicked, Beorn hospitable) but as the quest moves nearer to the Lonely Mountain this pattern starts to break down, and we are led to question our faith in the dwarves themselves.

The dwarves are, after Bilbo, the most fully described creatures in the book. One criticism which may be levelled at *The Hobbit* is that Tolkien fails to discriminate between the dwarves to any significant extent. We are given quite a distinct portrait of Thorin, and we know something of the characters of Kili, Fili, Bombur, and Balin; but the other dwarves are not individualised. They seem to be there simply to make up the number.

In *The Hobbit* the dwarves are given many of the characteristics one would associate with men. They may live longer lives but they are not immortal, and they have no supernatural power to free them from the adversaries that they encounter. In this respect the presentation of the dwarves is similar to that of the elves and the hobbits, and the fact that all these creatures behave so much as we do contributes to the success of Tolkien's description of their encounter at the Lonely Mountain. If any of these races were portrayed as obviously monstrous we would have no difficulty in deciding where our sympathies lay. The fact that all sides are so reasonable makes their confrontation more complex and more interesting.

The dwarves are presented positively in the early chapters of the book: they have music, and they are entertaining guests for Bilbo Baggins. In contrast, the trolls are presented as totally uncivilised. Like Bilbo they are greedy for food, but not for any of the conventional dishes which Bilbo and the dwarves enjoy: hobbits and dwarves eat as we do, but trolls eat anything at all, even dwarves. Furthermore, they speak in a vulgar and debased way, whereas the language of the hobbits and dwarves is based upon the standards of educated English. We may feel some disquiet here about Tolkien's method of presentation: he might seem to imply that, in real life, those who speak badly or who have poor table-manners are not to be trusted, whereas those with the leisure for second breakfasts and a taste for coloured waistcoats are likely to be in the right. Tolkien has been criticised for his apparent prejudice against the working class (remember what he says of coal-miners elsewhere in the book) and for the fact that *The Hobbit* is dominated by male characters.* It might be argued, against the latter charge, that medieval quests were generally undertaken by men; but they were addressed, quite clearly, to a very different reading public. The twentieth-century reader might have misgivings about the presentation of the trolls.

Nevertheless, by the end of the second chapter of *The Hobbit*, we have been given quite a positive portrait of the dwarves, and we are not required to question the fact that they steal from the trolls. The trolls have none of our sympathy and are defeated by their stupidity and their truculent nature. They are quarrelling even before Bilbo disturbs them, and Gandalf has only to exploit this tendency to cause their downfall.

Chapter 3, however, should make the reader more wary, and temper his response to the dwarves, because here we are introduced to the elves, who are presented as welcoming hosts and charming companions (if a little playful) but who are not liked by the dwarves: 'Dwarves don't get on well with them. Even decent enough dwarves like Thorin and his friends think them foolish' (Chapter 3). Elrond, chief of the elves, is the first character in the book to disapprove of the quest: 'he did not altogether approve of dwarves and their love of gold' (Chapter 3). It will be a sign of Bilbo's maturity when he shares this disquiet: he is not yet alive to the full implications of the quest.

*C.R. STIMPSON: *J.R.R. Tolkien*, Columbia University Press, New York, 1969, p.19.

After this encounter with a group of welcoming creatures, Thorin and company again meet with foes, but the goblins are not presented as simply as the trolls. The goblins are not ogres who can be turned to stone; they have their own history, which involves an uneasy relationship with the dwarves. The dispute between dwarves and goblins in Chapter 4 is presented as part of a continuing war between different but comparable races, with similar social systems, similar ways of fighting, but different values.

Just as the dwarves are helped by creatures of the natural world, in the shape of the eagles, so the goblins are in league with the Wargs. Tolkien himself wrote of the 'desire of men to hold communion with other living things' as one of the primal desires of men, and one which could be realised in fairy-stories.* This desire is realised in *The Hobbit* not only by the dwarves, but also by the goblins, who are in league with one of the most vicious of natural species. Together the goblins and the Wargs are working towards a plan which has nothing to do with the dwarves' quest. They intend to destroy the woodmen's village. This plan is frustrated by the turn of events, but the woodmen are never made aware of the danger from which they have been saved. For the first time in the book we are made to realise that there are other things going on in the world of this book aside from the dwarves' quest. We see that it is possible for major events to take place while large parts of the world remain untouched by them. The woodmen sleep on in their ignorance just as the hobbits in Hobbiton, at the end of the book, are never to learn of Bilbo's adventure.

After the dangers of the goblins and the Wargs, Bilbo and the dwarves again find friends who will feed them. The eagles are quite different from Elrond's elves. They are not kindly and, indeed, Bilbo wonders if they intend to keep him prisoner, or even eat him. Although the dwarves are fed by the eagles, their resting place hardly has the comfort of Rivendell.

The next creature introduced into the book is ambiguous in almost every respect. He is a shape-changer, at times a bear, at times a man; he can be a good host, but he is suspicious of strangers and refuses to believe Gandalf's tale until he has verified all the details himself. Beorn is completely in tune with nature: his very name is derived from an Old English word which meant both 'warrior' and 'bear'; it includes, furthermore, the element 'beo' which was the Old English word for bee, and the adventurers have to pass through bee-pastures before they arrive at Beorn's house. Beorn is attended by wonderful animals and, most significantly, he has no love of gold: '[The dwarves] spoke most of gold and silver and jewels and the making of things by smith-craft, and

*'On Fairy-Stories' in *Tree and Leaf*, Allen & Unwin, London, 1964, p.20.

Beorn did not appear to care for such things: there were no things of gold or silver in his hall, and few save the knives were made of metal at all' (Chapter 7). Again there is an implied criticism of the love of gold, and of the whole basis of the quest, from a character whom we are invited to respect and admire.

Although the battle with the spiders in Mirkwood raises no moral problems nor questions about what the dwarves are doing, the narrative line becomes more complex as the quest moves to the edge of Mirkwood. The dwarves are captured by elves, and we have been led to feel very positively about elves earlier in the book. There we were told that Elrond disapproved of dwarves, but here a more detailed cause is given for the dispute between dwarves and elves: 'In ancient days they had had wars with some of the dwarves, whom they accused of stealing their treasure' (Chapter 8). We are immediately given the dwarves' own version of the reason for the quarrel, which is very similar to the basis of the dispute between elves and dwarves at the end of *The Hobbit*: a dispute over the sharing of a treasure. We are shown for the first time that the dwarves' quest might be having a disturbing effect on the lives of other creatures: as far as the Elvenking is concerned, the dwarves have been attacking his people, and nothing Thorin says can convince him otherwise. By this stage of the book we should be aware that the rightness of Thorin's cause is being undermined: the quest can hardly be entirely good if Thorin is unable to admit to this true purpose. It is the Elvenking, wise as he is, who is the first to realise that the quest cannot end with the arrival of the dwarves at the Lonely Mountain:

'Very well! We'll see! No treasure will come back through Mirkwood without my having something to say in the matter' (Chapter 10).

By the time the Elvenking utters these words the quest has already altered. The dwarves have not yet realised that they will need the co-operation of the elves to get the treasure through Mirkwood, but they have begun to appreciate that they may be required to do more than merely steal the treasure. Thorin has announced himself in the Lake-town as 'Thorin, son of Thrain son of Thror, King under Mountain' and his motive has changed. He is no longer aiming to regain the treasure but now intends also to destroy Smaug and to become king. Only Bilbo is thoroughly unhappy as they approach the Lonely Mountain.

Smaug is the most potent adversary in the book. His physical size is immense, enough to enable him to destroy the Lake-town, but it is matched by an equally powerful intellect. The story of a dragon who guards a treasure is one with which Tolkien would be very familiar, since it occurs in *Beowulf*. In that poem the dragon's hoard is plundered and the dragon wakes into a fury which causes the destruction of innocent people. Beowulf is called upon to kill the dragon, but he himself perishes in this final act of bravery. There are clear differences between this story and Tolkien's use of the motif in *The Hobbit*; but it is notable that Bilbo, like Beowulf, approaches the dragon with false confidence. Bilbo has already had victories in the book and he misjudges the strength of the dragon. In the case of Bilbo, however, this lack of judgement does not prove fatal. One of the differences between the dragon in *Beowulf* and that in *The Hobbit* is that Smaug is described in much greater detail. The conversation he has with Bilbo is far more dangerous to the hobbit than the riddles of Gollum. Smaug is clever enough to sow suspicion in Bilbo's mind, to make his trust in the dwarves seem naive and misplaced:

> 'I suppose they are skulking outside, and your job is to do all the dangerous work and get what you can when I'm not looking—for them? And you will get a fair share? Don't you believe it! If you get off alive, you will be lucky!' (Chapter 12).

Smaug is skilful in his use of language. We have seen Gandalf use this same trick, more crudely (earlier in the book) to breed division among the trolls. This, however, is much more sophisticated, and had been deliberately prepared for by Tolkien. Throughout the book we have been increasingly concerned with the transformation of a simple adventure into something more complex: we have encountered characters who have either challenged the basis of the quest (like Elrond and Beorn) or the likelihood of its success (like the Elvenking) and now these challenges culminate in the words of Smaug, which make even Bilbo question what he is doing: 'I don't know if it has occurred to you that, even if you could steal the gold bit by bit . . . you could not get it very far? Not much use on the mountain-side? Not much use in the forest?' (Chapter 12). It is impossible to eat gold, as Thorin finds to his cost when he is besieged in the Lonely Mountain after Smaug's death. His very 'wealth' has alienated him from those whose help he most needs if he is ever to leave the mountain. The early chapters may have included alternating friends and foes; but whereas it was possible before for Thorin to look for welcome and an open-handed host, he will not be helped now unless he repays that earlier generosity. The debate which takes place at the Front Gate of the Lonely Mountain reflects no credit at all on Thorin. The claims of Bard and the Elvenking are reasonable, and Thorin's stubbornness might well have led to the destruction of all of the dwarves. It raises grave questions about his leadership which will be dealt with in more detail in the next section. That wholesale slaughter is averted is due partly to the arrival of the goblins and partly to Bilbo's last act of burglary: his theft of the Arkenstone.

There can be little doubt that Bilbo's taking of the Arkenstone is to be regarded as theft, but more significant than the theft is the fact that he uses his treasure for a proper end and is able, reluctantly, to renounce it. The importance of the Arkenstone has been explained to Bilbo before he enters Smaug's lair for the third time. Therefore, however much he may claim later that he took it only as his share of the treasure, there can be no question but that he was consciously stealing from the dwarves: 'Now I am a burglar indeed . . . But I suppose I must tell the dwarves about it—some time' (Chapter 13).

The Arkenstone is more than a jewel, it is a representation of kingship. It is appropriate that Bilbo should possess it for a time, because he has shown leadership in being prepared to enter Smaug's lair when none of the dwarves had courage enough. Yet Bilbo is able to renounce the stone and to give both the treasure and the power which it represents to Bard, because he can see that only Bard can overcome the corrupt Thorin.

Even Thorin, however, does not remain corrupt, although he is for a time unable to discriminate between friend and foe. His dying words of reconciliation with Bilbo effectively sum up one of the book's major themes, and show that Bilbo is not the only character to have matured during the quest: 'If more of us valued food and cheer and song above hoarded gold, it would be a merrier world' (Chapter 18).

# Kings and Masters

*The Hobbit* introduces various kinds of creatures as the quest progresses. It also presents us with a range of leaders and investigates the issue of what makes an effective king.

At the beginning of the book there appears to be no doubt about who is the leader of the company. Thorin Oakenshield arrives last of all the dwarves, and is treated with great deference by all of the company. He is, however, somewhat inferior in his powers to Gandalf. Gandalf is a wizard and has magical powers: he may not be the majestic figure who is to play such a central role in *The Lord of the Rings*, but he does have authority, and is able to extricate the company from danger on more than one occasion in the early part of the book. In the absence of Gandalf the dwarves increasingly look to Bilbo to give the lead, and this is not entirely because he has the magic ring. Although this ring proves a useful servant for Bilbo, it is his ingenuity and courage which enables him to take the lead. His rescue of the dwarves from the spiders and from the dungeons of the Elvenking require him to use both of these attributes, and the latter incident forces him to find special reserves of bravery to overcome his own fear of the water.

It might be argued that fortune plays a large part in Bilbo's success; but he clearly deserves his good luck. It is appropriate that he should, for example, find the magic ring, for he has the capacity to use it wisely. As Bilbo becomes more mature and more adept at leadership, so Thorin's authority becomes more questionable. Bilbo does not start the book with any illusions about his own social position or dignity, and this humility is one of his most attractive characteristics. Thorin, on the other hand, has a keen awareness of his status, and high expectations of how others should behave towards him. This haughtiness is increased by the way is hailed by the men of Esgaroth as the new king, and it almost becomes his downfall.

The Elvenking, the Master, and Bard all add to the analysis of leadership in *The Hobbit*. The Master is shrewd but selfish: he is wary of the arrival of Thorin because he has no wish to upset the Elvenking, with whom he trades. He tries to save himself rather than his people when Smaug is destroying the town, but he is clever enough as an orator to persuade the people not to depose him in favour of Bard. Ultimately he comes to a bad end and dies alone and exiled. His career is an example of the corrupt leadership of a man who refuses to see that he has a duty to his people equal to the allegiance he expects from them.

Bard the bowman seems an appropriate selection as a leader. He is perceptive enough to realise that the fire from the Lonely Mountain signifies the wrath of the dragon and not the victory of Thorin, and he proves a decisive general when Smaug arrives at Esgaroth. He has, moreover, a direct claim to leadership in that he is descended from Girion, Lord of Dale, and is set apart from other men by his gift of communication with the birds. Although he is generally described in positive terms, he is not without his faults: at the siege of the Lonely Mountain he has to be restrained from open warfare by the calming influence of the Elvenking: 'Long will I tarry, ere I begin this war for gold' (Chapter 17).

The words of the Elvenking may well come as a surprise since he is first introduced to us as an enemy of the dwarves, and hence not a character with whom we are invited to sympathise. In the course of the novel as a whole, however, we are increasingly led to see that the Elvenking may have reason to imprison the dwarves and that his conduct is almost always based upon shrewd reason.

The debate which takes place at the Front Gate of the Lonely Mountain in Chapter 15 owes a great deal to an Old English poem in which Tolkien was particularly interested: *The Battle of Maldon*. In this poem two armies confront each other and their conflict is preceded by formal speeches which are similar in tone to those exchanged by Bard and Thorin. In *The Battle of Maldon* the leader of the English army, Beorhtnoth, yields too much land to the opposing forces as a result of his own misplaced pride. Because of this error Beorhtnoth and his army perish. *The Battle of Maldon* so interested Tolkien that he wrote a poem

'The Homecoming of Beorhtnoth Beorhthelm's Son' which continues the narrative of the Old English poem, and which condemns Beorhtnoth's folly. Thorin, in *The Hobbit*, demonstrates a similar arrogance, which springs in his case from a lust for gold rather than from a lust for glory, but which could easily have led to the destruction of his followers. It is more than a coincidence that Thorin promises peace but plans treacherously to continue the conflict, just as Gollum has done earlier in the book.

## The ring

The ring that Bilbo found in the dark tunnels under the Misty Mountains became the central object in Tolkien's trilogy *The Lord of the Rings*. It does not have so central a role in *The Hobbit*, nor does it exercise the power of the One Ring in the later work. It renders the wearer invisible, and it is inclined to play tricks—as, for example, when it slips from Bilbo's finger as he is escaping from the Misty Mountains—but it does not exercise any power over the mind of the owner. Bilbo is in more danger of being corrupted by the Arkenstone than he is by wearing the ring. Indeed it is sometimes not clear when Bilbo is wearing the ring and when he has taken it off, so little does it affect him. The reader may be puzzled about whether Bilbo takes off the ring before releasing the dwarves from the barrels at Esgaroth, for example: in *The Lord of the Rings* so terrible is the power of the ring that it could not be worn in this casual manner.

## The past

*The Hobbit* is essentially a nostalgic work, looking back to a past which was better than today. It is set long ago 'when there was less noise and more green' and the whole tone of the book is coloured by this setting. Although the creatures in the book may be invented or mythological, its landscape is that of rural England: it is from this setting that Bilbo comes, and to it that he returns. His movements on the quest are charted in terms of the progression of the seasons in England, the natural cycle of the country year. Tolkien is not the first to write of a dragon laying waste to all the ground around his lair, but his use of that detail may be significant. Smaug is evil and his wickedness is clear from the fact that his very presence causes all natural growth to stop: he stores up property to no productive effect and prevents the land being put to its proper use. With the death of Smaug, the land is re-planted and peace returns to Dale.

It is tempting to regard all this as an allegory, especially in the light of the treatment of the countryside in the book as a whole. Smaug could be taken to represent the worst excesses of greed and the pointless amassing of capital, effectively stifling the opportunity for ordinary people to earn their living. When Smaug dies trade increases, and Esgaroth prospers:

> 'The new Master is of a wiser kind,' said Balin, 'and very popular, for, of course, he gets most of the credit for the present prosperity. They are making songs which say that in his days the rivers run with gold.'
> 'Then the prophecies of the old songs have turned out to be true, after a fashion!' said Bilbo. (Chapter 19)

The prophecies turn out to be true, and it would be a foolish reader who scoffed at dragons after the lesson of *The Hobbit*.

# Part 4

# Hints for study

Most students of *The Hobbit* will be preparing to answer essay questions for examinations. Questions on the book will define quite precisely what aspect is to be written about (there are some sample essay topics included in this text): it is clearly impossible for any student to write all that they know of *The Hobbit* in a single essay.

Questions asked about novels tend to be on one of three areas:

(a) Character
(b) Incident
(c) Themes

These three divisions are not totally separate, but it will be helpful to treat each category individually in order to make clear the kind of answer which is being required.

## Character study

The reader of novels or plays is initially interested in the characters of the participants. Indeed the success of a novel or play may well rest in the reader's ability to understand why a particular character behaves in the way that he does: to sympathise with the character.

To write a study of a character in *The Hobbit* you need to establish the following points:

(1) List the situations in which the character appears
(2) Note what is said by the character
(3) Note what is said to the character
(4) Note what is said about the character (either by the narrator, or by other characters in the book)
(5) Note what is said about the character in those incidents in which the character does not appear
(6) Note the way in which the character might change or develop in the course of the book

Not all characters are equally significant in the book, and you need to bear this in mind in tackling an essay question. Bilbo Baggins is obviously the central character, the one who says and does most in the book, and the one who changes most. It is unlikely that an essay question would require a full character study of Bilbo: the subject is simply too large. Questions on Bilbo will probably ask for an investigation of his behaviour in a particular incident. However, it is quite possible that a question on a lesser character like Beorn would require a full discussion of the role he plays throughout the book.

It is easy to forget that Tolkien chooses to tell the story from Bilbo's point of view: by making the hobbit the central character Tolkien manipulates and directs our sympathy and interest. You might usefully consider how different the novel would be if it had been written from the point of view of, for example, Bofur, or Bard. Such a task can reveal a great deal about the way in which a novel works.

The sample essay topics in this book all deal exclusively with *The Hobbit* and this will be true of examination essay titles in general. The student who had, however, looked at the opening chapters of *The Lord of the Rings* and who therefore knew how Tolkien went on to develop the story of Gollum and the magic ring, might well be able to employ this knowledge to advantage in his essays.

Bilbo is the central character in the novel, and the most fully developed. This means that we see him in enough different situations in the course of the book to establish how he changes as a result of his adventures. You might find it a useful aid to understanding the workings of *The Hobbit* to ask yourself the following questions:

(1) What do we know of Bilbo at the beginning of the book?
(2) How does any particular incident change Bilbo?
(3) How is this change in character made clear to the reader?

Very often the answer to the third question will involve a reference to another character: a particular incident will have one effect upon Bilbo and an entirely different effect upon another character. For example, Bard's statement at the Lonely Mountain about his claim to a share of the treasure affects Thorin and Bilbo quite differently, and this difference is a measure of their separate characters. A good deal of the work that a student does on a character in a novel involves comparison with other characters and the sample essay topics reflect this fact.

It will not be possible to apply the questions above to all characters in the book: a large number do not play a large enough part to enable them to be developed (Bolg, for example, the King of the Goblins, appears on only one occasion). *The Hobbit* has one particular feature not found in most other novels, which requires us to extend our treatment of character. Most works of literature are concerned with a single species (man); Tolkien fills *The Hobbit* with different kinds of creatures and therefore raises questions which require us to compare, for example, elves with dwarves.

To do this we can simply take the list of questions on p.62 and apply them to a race of creatures rather than to single individuals.

## Plot and incident

In the section above it should be clear that questions on character cannot be identified without reference to incident: character is revealed through activity in a particular incident. To study particular incidents, therefore, requires only a shift in perspective and a slightly different list of questions. To decide, for example, what is the significance of the escape from the Elvenking's fortress, we need to establish:

(1) Who is involved in the incident?
(2) What do they do and say?
(3) What is said about them?
(4) (As a result of the answers to the first three questions) how can this incident be shown to have different effects on different characters?
(5) Are there incidents elsewhere in the book which are similar to this one (for example, other kinds of imprisonment for the dwarves)? If so, how is this incident different?

## Themes

Any work of literature will inevitably be concerned with more than simply telling a story. Although an initial interest may be stirred by the characters and what happens to those characters, the enduring appeal of a text must reside in more than this: the text must have certain themes.

There is a particular kind of literature in which the themes matter more than the characters, in which the characters are there simply to represent particular issues or qualities such as Wrath or Revenge: this technique is called allegory and it is found in, for example, English plays of the medieval period. Tolkien himself wrote: 'I cordially dislike allegory in all its manifestations, and always have done so since I grew old and wary enough to detect its presence.' We should be wary, therefore, of treating *The Hobbit* as allegory but, nevertheless, be alive to the themes it contains and the issues it raises.

We can investigate these quite simply by asking of the characters in the book:

(1) What kinds of life do these characters lead?
(2) What motives lead them to act as they do (for example, greed, selfishness, concern for others)?
(3) Are we to respond sympathetically or unsympathetically to these actions?

As an example of this we might take the instances of Thorin and the Elvenking. Our attitudes to these two characters change in the course of the novel, not because the characters develop but because we, the readers, develop in our understanding of their motives. We become increasingly uneasy about Thorin's behaviour and his motives as he gets closer to Smaug's treasure, and even more uneasy when he has gained possession of it. In comparison, however, our impression of the Elvenking grows more positive: we appreciate that he may have had reasons for imprisoning the dwarves; we see him being ready to help rebuild the Lake-town; we approve of his joining forces with Bard (because we respect Bard).

One of the strengths of *The Hobbit* is that its characters do not behave in a simple uniform way throughout the novel, and our response to their motives is often linked with the way in which those motives reveal particular themes: greed; concern for others; fear; desire for a better life; the wish for comfort. It is no accident that in the Battle of Five Armies, victory is only possible when the forces of civilisation are prepared to suspend their petty quarrels and recognise the need to fight together against a common evil.

## Sample essay questions

(1) Compare any two episodes in *The Hobbit* in which Bilbo is required to act on his own initiative and demonstrate how each reveals different aspects of his character.
(2) In what ways are we prepared for Thorin's greed?
(3) What are the principal differences in character between the elves and the dwarves?
(4) Describe the events which lead up to the destruction of Esogareth *or* the Battle of the Five Armies.
(5) Compare and contrast the characters of the Elvenking and the Master.
(6) Write briefly on three of the following: The Arkenstone, Beorn, Wargs, Rivendell, Roäc.
(7) How is Bilbo made to seem an unsuitable partner for the dwarves in Chapter 1 of *The Hobbit*?
(8) 'If more of us valued food and cheer and song above hoarded gold, it would be a merrier world'. In what ways is *The Hobbit* concerned with a struggle between those who value food and cheer and those who hoard gold?
(9) What do we learn of Gollum and Bilbo in their confrontation in Chapter 5 of *The Hobbit*?
(10) Discuss the reasons why Gandalf needs to leave the party from time to time.

---

**Model answer to question (9)**

---

*In order to demonstrate the way in which a particular essay question might be approached, there follows a model answer for question nine in the list above. After this essay you will find an explanation of why it takes the form it does.*

Bilbo is separated from his companions in the tunnels beneath the Misty Mountains. He falls from the back of Dori, who has been carrying him, and is knocked unconscious. The first test to his character, when he comes to his senses, is the temptation to panic in the face of darkness and isolation. In the earlier episodes of the adventure Bilbo has always been with the dwarves, and his courage here in being able to act alone without fear prepares us for the initiatives that Bilbo has to undertake later in the book.

He walks on through the dark tunnels until he steps into water. At this point we are told of Bilbo's fear of water and of the creatures living in the water. He has not yet gained the courage necessary to overcome that fear, but he will display that courage very soon in rescuing the dwarves from the stronghold of the Elvenking. At the moment, however, Bilbo stops by the edge of the pool.

Gollum, who lives in the pool, is surprised to see Bilbo and wonders what kind of a creature he is. Like many other characters in the book, Gollum is unsure about the hobbit: hobbits are not normally found outside of their homelands, and the other creatures of the world are uncertain what they can do. It is this uncertainty that stops Gollum killing Bilbo immediately.

Instead they play a riddle game, and here Bilbo is able to display his ingenuity and his resourcefulness. He has to answer Gollum's riddles and invent some of his own. Later on in the book Bilbo is to be involved in a similar contest with Smaug, another creature who is not certain about the nature of hobbits: this riddle-game proves to be useful practice for him. However, Bilbo does not succeed entirely through his own efforts. When he is almost defeated, unable to answer one of Gollum's riddles, a fish falls on to his toes and gives him the answer; and later, when he really has given up, he tries to ask for more time but is unable to utter more than the single word 'Time!': this is the answer. The book as a whole shows Bilbo succeeding through a combination of good judgement and good fortune: this is appropriate for one who was invited on to the quest to make a lucky number.

Although Bilbo is fortunate in being able to find the answer to Gollum's questions, he does not behave dishonestly, and this distinguishes him from Gollum. After he has failed to defeat Bilbo in the riddle-game, Gollum tries a different strategy: he tells Bilbo that he must ask a question. Gollum tries to cheat here by having more than three guesses, and, even more seriously, when he has to acknowledge defeat, he still plans to kill Bilbo if he can.

Gollum's attitude to the ring, which he hopes to use to defeat Bilbo, is very revealing. It is not made clear in this book how Gollum came to have the ring, but what is very clear is the effect it has upon him. It used to tire him to wear it, but now it galls him: he has invented a story to explain to himself why he has it; and he is fiercely possessive in his desire to retain control of it.

Many characters in *The Hobbit* are excessively greedy even when (as in the case of Smaug) they gain no profit or pleasure from their possessions except in depriving others of owning them. Even Bilbo shows signs of this vice, later in the book, in his reluctance to part with the Arkenstone. Gollum's ring is unlike the Arkenstone, or the treasure in the Lonely Mountain, for it is magic and it seems to have the power to make its owner particularly jealous and greedy. This power is explained more fully in *The Lord of the Rings*.

Bilbo uses the ring (by accident again) to avoid the wrath of Gollum and to follow him as he rushes through the tunnels towards the door. When they reach the end of the tunnel Bilbo displays the aspect of his character which most distinguishes him from Gollum: he feels pity for his adversary. As Gollum stands in front of him, blocking his path and yet unable to see him, Bilbo's first reaction is to 'stab the foul thing, put its eyes out, kill it'. But he goes on to think of Gollum's plight, to imagine what a dreadful life the poor creature leads. He understands the loneliness, the darkness, and the boredom in which Gollum lives, and he decides to jump over Gollum rather than to kill him.

There are instances later in the book of Bilbo's willingness to understand the viewpoint of someone else: in particular Bilbo appreciates that Bard has a real claim to a share of Smaug's treasure. Thorin is blinded by his own selfishness, but Bilbo has the imagination to think of how other people might see the situation.

Thus it is appropriate that Bilbo should escape from the dangers of the tunnels and be able to rejoin his companions. He has shown courage, intelligence, pity, honesty, and had the benefit of a share of good fortune. Gollum, by contrast, has tried to cheat, has attempted to misuse the power which he had, and must go back to his pool, filled with hatred and despair, totally alone.

This answer was written from the plan below:

(a) Bilbo before he meets Gollum: dark, alone
(b) Bilbo's fear of water: Barrels out of Bonds
(c) Gollum unsure of hobbits: like others (Smaug)
(d) Riddle game: Smaug again; Bilbo's cleverness; luck on Bilbo's side

(e) Honesty: Gollum dishonest
(f) Ring: kinds of greed: deceiving self
(g) Bilbo pities Gollum: Gollum hates him
(h) Bilbo outwits the goblins
(i) Bilbo avoids the sunshine: evil of ring?

In both the plan and the finished essay each incident in Bilbo's meeting with Gollum is commented upon. It would be insufficient to point out that the two play a riddle-game: we must indicate what this reveals of their characters. This particular question requires the writer to focus upon one part of the novel, but since the question is concerned with character, some reference to other parts of the book is inevitable. The essential point to bear in mind is not to write so much about the rest of the book that there is not enough space to treat the episode in question in sufficient detail. An essay which started: 'When we first meet Bilbo Baggins he is standing by his door after breakfast, smoking his pipe. Gandalf comes up to him and Bilbo says "Good morning"'—and which went on to describe the first meeting between Gandalf and Bilbo, would not be adequate as an answer to this particular question.

The structure of both the plan and the essay is determined by the sequence of events in the narrative: each aspect of the incident is dealt with in the order in which it occurs, and each is commented upon in the light of what is revealed about the two characters. Notice that the final essay omits some of the points listed in the plan: it does not include, for example, any reference to Bilbo's ability to outwit the goblins. Although this episode is part of the incident mentioned in the question, it does not reveal any aspect of Bilbo's character which has not been commented upon earlier in the essay.

## Making comparisons

It should be evident that *The Hobbit* is written in such a way as to require the reader to make comparisons of various kinds. We are led to compare the attitudes of different characters in the same situation; to compare similar incidents; to compare similar physical settings. It might be helpful to draw up a list of possible comparisons which may be useful at a later stage in writing an examination answer.

For example, you might list dangerous situations in the book: stealing from the trolls; being captured by the goblins; meeting Gollum; being attacked by Wargs, etc. A similar list could be compiled of welcoming situations, and each of these lists could be modified slightly to emphasise character rather than incident: thus you could have, on the one hand, a list of foes and, on the other, a list of friends. If you read Part 3 closely you will find material which will help you in compiling these lists.

# Part 5

# Suggestions for further reading

## The text

The text used in these Notes is the edition of 1972, with an introduction by R.S. Fowler, published by Allen & Unwin, London.

## Other works by Tolkien

All Tolkien's fiction and verse is published in England by Allen & Unwin, and in the U.S.A. by Houghton Mifflin. His major work, the trilogy *The Lord of the Rings*, was first published in a single volume in 1966.

Two other works by Tolkien are particularly relevant for the study of *The Hobbit*:

'On Fairy-Stories' in *Tree and Leaf*, Allen and Unwin, London, 1964.
'Beowulf: The Monsters and the Critics', Oxford University Press, London, 1937.

## Biography

CARPENTER, H.: *J. R. R. Tolkien: A Biography*, Allen & Unwin, London, 1977. The authoritative biography. This full and readable account of Tolkien's life and work includes a bibliography of all of his writings. It can sometimes be frustrating because it does not cite the sources of many of the quotations attributed to Tolkien.
CARPENTER, H.: *The Inklings*, Allen & Unwin, London, 1978. This is an account of the Oxford literary circle of which Tolkien was a member.

## Reference guides

FOSTER, R.: *The Complete Guide to Middle Earth*, Allen & Unwin, London, 1978; and
TYLER, J.E.A.: *The Tolkien Companion*, Macmillan, London, 1975. Each of these works is an alphabetically arranged guide to the names of people, places, creatures, events, and objects in Tolkien's fiction. Neither makes much attempt to refer his work to a wider context.

NOEL, R.S.: *The Mythology of Middle-Earth*, Thames & Hudson, London, 1977. This book attempts to note the parallels between Tolkien's invented mythology and the myths and legends of Northern Europe. It is much less substantial than such a topic deserves, although its glossary of names in Tolkien is valuable.

## Criticism of The Hobbit

WEST, R.C.: *Tolkien Criticism: An Annotated Checklist*, Kent State University Press, Kent, Ohio, 1970. This is a comprehensive list of Tolkien criticism, most of which is concerned with *The Lord of the Rings*.

HELMS, R.: *Tolkien's World*, Thames & Hudson, London, 1974. The second chapter of this book is a sound comparison of *The Hobbit* and *The Lord of the Rings*. Chapter 3 is more far-fetched: it is a Freudian account of *The Hobbit*.

KOCHER, P.: *Master of Middle-Earth*, Thames & Hudson, London, 1972. Chapter 2 deals sensibly with the way *The Hobbit* is more than a children's story.

NITZCHE, J.C.: *Tolkien's Art*, Macmillan, London, 1979. This book has some revealing insights but it also includes some bizarre observations (Bilbo is said to be a Christ figure). It has a comprehensive bibliography.

## Background reading

A reading of *The Hobbit* will be enhanced by an acquaintance with Old English literature. A useful anthology of modern English translation of Old English verse is:

GORDON, R.K. (ED.): *Anglo-Saxon Poetry*, Dent, London, 1926.

# The author of these notes

GEOFFREY RIDDEN was educated at the University of Leeds where he completed a research degree on Milton's *Samson Agonistes* before taking up a lectureship at the University of Ghana. After returning to England he held posts at the University of Durham, Westfield College, London, and University College, London. Since 1976 he has been a Senior Lecturer in English at King Alfred's College, Winchester, and Acting Course Director of the B.A. English degree programmes. He has published a number of articles and reviews, principally on Milton and aspects of linguistics, as well as composing the scores for three musicals.